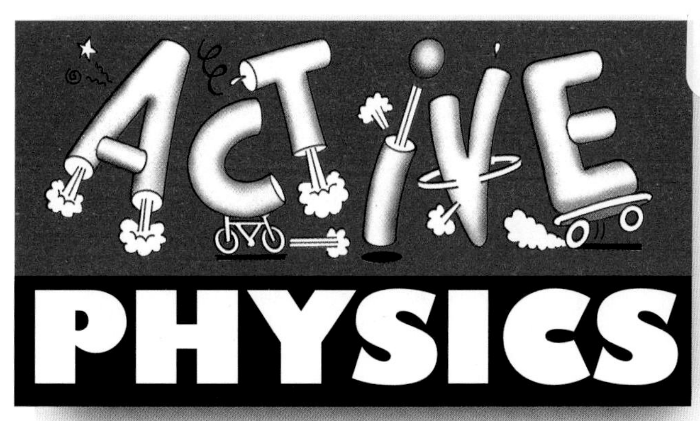

Arthur Eisenkraft, Ph.D.

Active Physics has been developed in association
with the
American Association of Physics Teachers (AAPT)
and the
American Institute of Physics (AIP)

Published by
IT'S ABOUT TIME, Inc.
Armonk, NY

Published in 2000 by

It's About Time, Inc.
84 Business Park Drive, Armonk, NY 10504
Phone (914) 273-2233 Fax (914) 273-2227
Toll Free (888) 698-TIME
www.ITS-ABOUT-TIME.com

Publisher
Laurie Kreindler

Project Manager
Ruta Demery

Design
John Nordland

Production Manager
Barbara Zahm

Creative Artwork
Tomas Bunk

Cover Illustration
Steven Belcher

Technical Art
Burmar

Illustrations and Photos
Tomas Bunk pages 4, 12, 18, 24, 30, 36, 43, 49, 54, 64, 69, 74, 80, 86, 91, 101, 110, 116, 121, 126, 133, 139, 145, 150, 155; Photos: page 17 Courtesy of Steinway & Sons, page 99 by Mekea Z. Hurwitz, Courtesy of The Riverdale Press, page 123 Courtesy of National Space Science Data Center, all other photos by PhotoDisc Inc.

All student activities in this textbook have been designed to be as safe as possible, and have been reviewed by professionals specifically for that purpose. As well, appropriate warnings concerning potential safety hazards are included where applicable to particular activities. However, responsibility for safety remains with the student, the classroom teacher, the school principal, and the school board.

Printed and bound in the United States of America

ISBN 1-891629-00-X (Softcover Edition) ISBN 1-891629-47-6 (Hardcover Edition)
ISBN 1-891629-43-3 (Softcover 6 unit set) ISBN 1-891629-53-0 (Hardcover 6 unit set)

2 3 4 5 D 02 01 00 99

This project was supported, in part, by the
National Science Foundation
Opinions expressed are those of the authors and not necessarily those of the Foundation

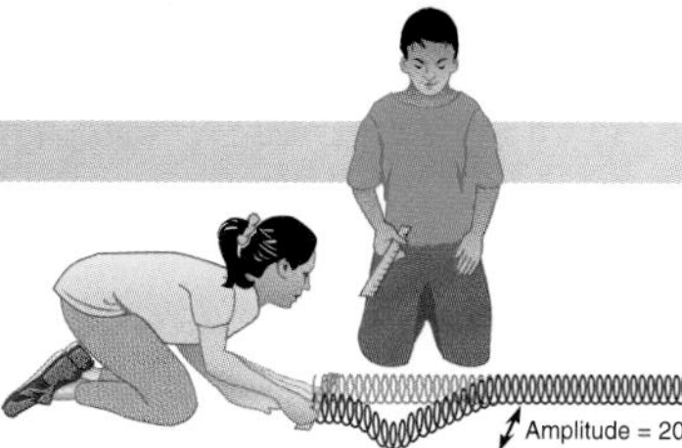

Communication

Table of Contents

Acknowledgments

Project Director

Arthur Eisenkraft teaches physics and serves as science coordinator in the Bedford Public Schools in N.Y. Dr. Eisenkraft is the author of numerous science and educational publications. He holds a US Patent for a laser vision testing system and was featured in *Scientific American*.

Dr. Eisenkraft is chair of the Duracell Science Scholarship Competition; chair of the Toyota TAPESTRY program giving grants to science teachers; and chair of the Toshiba/NSTA ExploraVisions Awards competition for grades K-12. He is co-author of a contest column and serves on the advisory board of *Quantum* magazine, a collaborative effort of the US and Russia. In 1993, he served as Executive Director for the XXIV International Physics Olympiad after being Academic Director for the United States Team for six years. He served on the content committee and helped write the National Science Education Standards of the NRC (National Research Council).

Dr. Eisenkraft received the Presidential Award for Excellence in Science Teaching at the White House in 1986, and the AAPT Distinguished Service Citation for "excellent contributions to the teaching of physics" in 1989. In 1991 he was recognized by the Disney Corporation as Science Teacher of the Year in their American Teacher Awards program. In 1993 he received an Honorary Doctor of Science degree from Rensselaer Polytechnic Institute and in 1999 was elected president of the National Science Teachers Association (NSTA).

Primary and Contributing Authors

Communication

Richard Berg
University of Maryland
College Park, MD

Ron DeFronzo
Eastbay Ed. Collaborative
Attleboro, MA

Harry Rheam
Eastern Senior High School
Atco, NJ

John Roeder
The Calhoun School
New York, NY

Patty Rourke
Potomac School
McLean, VA

Larry Weathers
The Bromfield School
Harvard, MA

Home

Jon L. Harkness
Active Physics Regional Coordinator
Wausau, WI

Douglas A. Johnson
Madison West High School
Madison, WI

John J. Rusch
University of Wisconsin, Superior
Superior, WI

Ruta Demery
Blue Ink Editing
Stayner, ON

Medicine

Russell Hobbie
University of Minnesota
St. Paul, MN

Terry Goerke
Hill-Murray High School
St. Paul, MN

John Koser
Wayzata High School
Plymouth, MN

Ed Lee
WonderScience, Associate Editor
Silver Spring, MD

Predictions

Ruth Howes
Ball State University
Muncie, IN

Chris Chiaverina
New Trier Township High School
Crystal Lake, IL

Charles Payne
Ball State University
Muncie, IN

Ceanne Tzimopoulos
Omega Publishing
Medford, MA

Sports

Howard Brody
University of Pennsylvania
Philadelphia, PA

Mary Quinlan
Radnor High School
Radnor, PA

Carl Duzen
Lower Merion High School
Havertown, PA

Jon L. Harkness
Active Physics Regional Coordinator
Wausau, WI

David Wright
Tidewater Comm. College
Virginia Beach, VA

Transportation

Ernest Kuehl
Lawrence High School
Cedarhurst, NY

Robert L. Lehrman
Bayside, NY

Salvatore Levy
Roslyn High School
Roslyn, NY

Tom Liao
SUNY Stony Brook
Stony Brook, NY

Bob Ritter
University of Alberta
Edmonton, AB, CA

Principal Investigators

Bernard V. Khoury
American Association of Physics Teachers

Dwight Edward Neuenschwander
American Institute of Physics

Consultants

Peter Brancazio
Brooklyn College of CUNY
Brooklyn, NY

Robert Capen
Canyon del Oro High School
Tucson, AZ

Carole Escobar

Earl Graf
SUNY Stony Brook
Stony Brook, NY

Jack Hehn
American Association of Physics Teachers
College Park, MD

Donald F. Kirwan
Louisiana State University
Baton Rouge, LA

Gayle Kirwan
Louisiana State University
Baton Rouge, LA

James La Porte
Virginia Tech
Blacksburg, VA

Charles Misner
University of Maryland
College Park, MD

Robert F. Neff
Suffern, NY

Ingrid Novodvorsky
Mountain View High School
Tucson, AZ

John Robson
University of Arizona
Tucson, AZ

Mark Sanders
Virginia Tech
Blacksburg, VA

Brian Schwartz
Brooklyn College of CUNY
New York, NY

Bruce Seiger
Wellesley High School
Newburyport, MA

Clifford Swartz
SUNY Stony Brook
Setauket, NY

Barbara Tinker
The Concord Consortium
Concord, MA

Robert E. Tinker
The Concord Consortium
Concord, MA

Joyce Weiskopf
Herndon, VA

Donna Willis
American Association of Physics Teachers
College Park, MD

Safety Reviewer

Gregory Puskar
University of West Virginia
Morgantown, WV

Equity Reviewer

Leo Edwards
Fayetteville State University
Fayetteville, NC

Spreadsheet and MBL

Ken Appel
Yorktown High School
Peekskill, NY

Physics at Work

Barbara Zahm
Zahm Productions
New York, NY

Physics InfoMall

Brian Adrian
Bethany College
Lindsborg, KS

Unit Reviewers

George A. Amann
F.D. Roosevelt High School
Rhinebeck, NY

Patrick Callahan
Catasaugua High School
Center Valley, PA

Beverly Cannon
Science and Engineering Magnet High School
Dallas, TX

Barbara Chauvin

Elizabeth Chesick
The Baldwin School
Haverford, PA 19041

Chris Chiaverina
New Trier Township High School
Crystal Lake, IL

Andria Erzberger
Palo Alto Senior High School
Los Altos Hills, CA

Elizabeth Farrell Ramseyer
Niles West High School
Skokie, IL

Mary Gromko
President of Council of State Science Supervisors
Denver, CO

Thomas Guetzloff

Jon L. Harkness
Active Physics Regional Coordinator
Wausau, WI

Dawn Harman
Moon Valley High School
Phoenix, AZ

James Hill
Piner High School
Sonoma, CA

Bob Kearney

Claudia Khourey-Bowers
McKinley Senior High School

Steve Kliewer
Bullard High School
Fresno, CA

Ernest Kuehl
Roslyn High School
Cedarhurst, NY

Jane Nelson
University High School
Orlando, FL

John Roeder
The Calhoun School
New York, NY

Patty Rourke
Potomac School
McLean, VA

Gerhard Salinger
Fairfax, VA

Irene Slater
La Pietra School for Girls

Pilot Test Teachers

John Agosta

Donald Campbell
Portage Central High School
Portage, MI

John Carlson
Norwalk Community
Technical College
Norwalk, CT

Veanna Crawford
Alamo Heights High School
New Braunfels

Janie Edmonds
West Milford High School
Randolph, NJ

Eddie Edwards
Amarillo Area Center for
Advanced Learning
Amarillo, TX

Arthur Eisenkraft
Fox Lane High School
Bedford, NY

Tom Ford

Bill Franklin

Roger Goerke
St. Paul, MN

Tom Gordon
Greenwich High School
Greenwich, CT

Ariel Hepp

John Herrman
College of Steubenville
Steubenville, OH

Linda Hodges

Ernest Kuehl
Lawrence High School
Cedarhurst, NY

Fran Leary
Troy High School
Schenectady, NY

Harold Lefcourt

Cherie Lehman
West Lafayette High School
West Lafayette, IN

Kathy Malone
Shady Side Academy
Pittsburgh, PA

Bill Metzler
Westlake High School
Thornwood, NY

Elizabeth Farrell Ramseyer
Niles West High School
Skokie, IL

Daniel Repogle
Central Noble High School
Albion, IN

Evelyn Restivo
Maypearl High School
Maypearl, TX

Doug Rich
Fox Lane High School
Bedford, NY

John Roeder
The Calhoun School
New York, NY

Tom Senior
New Trier Township High School
Highland Park, IL

John Thayer
District of Columbia Public Schools
Silver Spring, MD

Carol-Ann Tripp
Providence Country Day
East Providence, RI

Yvette Van Hise
High Tech High School
Freehold, NJ

Jan Waarvick

Sandra Walton
Dubuque Senior High School
Dubuque, IA

Larry Wood
Fox Lane High School
Bedford, NY

Field Test Coordinator

Marilyn Decker
Northeastern University
Acton, MA

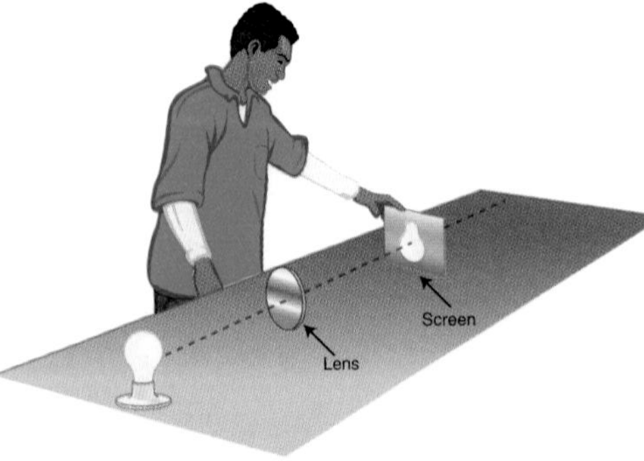

Field Test Workshop Staff

John Carlson

Marilyn Decker

Arthur Eisenkraft

Douglas Johnson

John Koser

Ernest Kuehl

Mary Quinlan

Elizabeth Farrell Ramseyer

John Roeder

Field Test Evaluators

Susan Baker-Cohen

Susan Cloutier

George Hein

Judith Kelley

all from Lesley College,
Cambridge, MA

Field Test Teachers and Schools

Rob Adams
Polytech High School
Woodside, DE

Benjamin Allen
Falls Church High School
Falls Church, VA

Robert Applebaum
New Trier High School
Winnetka, IL

Joe Arnett
Plano Sr. High School
Plano, TX

Bix Baker
GFW High School
Winthrop, MN

Debra Beightol
Fremont High School
Fremont, NE

Patrick Callahan
Catasaugua High School
Catasaugua, PA

George Coker
Bowling Green High School
Bowling Green, KY

Janice Costabile
South Brunswick High School
Monmouth Junction, NJ

Stanley Crum
Homestead High School
Fort Wayne, IN

Russel Davison
Brandon High School
Brandon, FL

Christine K. Deyo
Rochester Adams High School
Rochester Hills, MI

Jim Doller
Fox Lane High School
Bedford, NY

Jessica Downing
Esparto High School
Esparto, CA

Douglas Fackelman
Brighton High School
Brighton, CO

Rick Forrest
Rochester High School
Rochester Hills, MI

Mark Freeman
Blacksburg High School
Blacksburg, VA

Jonathan Gillis
Enloe High School
Raleigh, NC

Karen Gruner
Holton Arms School
Bethesda, MD

Larry Harrison
DuPont Manual High School
Louisville, KY

Alan Haught
Weaver High School
Hartford, CT

Steven Iona
Horizon High School
Thornton, CO

Phil Jowell
Oak Ridge High School
Conroe, TX

Deborah Knight
Windsor Forest High School
Savannah, GA

Thomas Kobilarcik
Marist High School
Chicago, IL

Sheila Kolb
Plano Senior High School
Plano, TX

Todd Lindsay
Park Hill High School
Kansas City, MO

Malinda Mann
South Putnam High School
Greencastle, IN

Steve Martin
Maricopa High School
Maricopa, AZ

Nancy McGrory
North Quincy High School
N. Quincy, MA

David Morton
Mountain Valley High School
Rumford, ME

Charles Muller
Highland Park High School
Highland Park, NJ

Fred Muller
Mercy High School
Burlingame, CA

Vivian O'Brien
Plymouth Regional High School
Plymouth, NH

Robin Parkinson
Northridge High School
Layton, UT

Donald Perry
Newport High School
Bellevue, WA

Francis Poodry
Lincoln High School
Philadelphia, PA

John Potts
Custer County District High School
Miles City, MT

Doug Rich
Fox Lane High School
Bedford, NY

John Roeder
The Calhoun School
New York, NY

Consuelo Rogers
Maryknoll Schools
Honolulu, HI

Lee Rossmaessler, Ph.D
Mott Middle College High School
Flint, MI

John Rowe
Hughes Alternative Center
Cincinnati, OH

Rebecca Bonner Sanders
South Brunswick High School
Monmouth Junction, NJ

David Schlipp
Narbonne High School
Harbor City, CA

Eric Shackelford
Notre Dame High School
Sherman Oaks, CA

Robert Sorensen
Springville-Griffith Institute and
Central School
Springville, NY

Teresa Stalions
Crittenden County High School
Marion, KY

Roberta Tanner
Loveland High School
Loveland, CO

Anthony Umelo
Anacostia Sr. High School
Washington, D.C.

Judy Vondruska
Mitchell High School
Mitchell, SD

Deborah Waldron
Yorktown High School
Arlington, VA

Ken Wester
The Mississippi School for
Mathematics and Science
Columbus, MS

Susan Willis
Conroe High School
Conroe, TX

You can do physics. Here are the reasons why.

The following features make it that much easier to understand the physics principles you will be studying. Using all these features together will help you actually learn about this subject and see how it works for you everyday, everywhere. Look for all these features in each chapter of Active Physics.

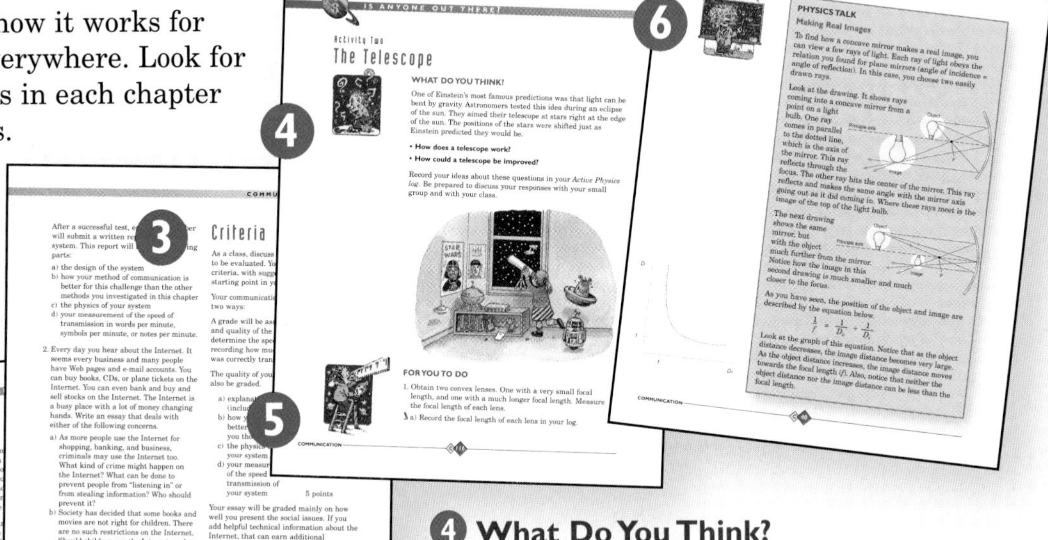

❶ Scenario

Each unit begins with a realistic event or situation you might actually have experienced, or can imagine yourself participating in at home, in school, or in your community.

❷ Challenge

This feature presents the problem you will soon be expected to solve, or the tasks you are expected to complete using the knowledge you gain in the chapter.

❸ Criteria

Before the chapter begins you will learn exactly how you will be graded. Working with your classmates, you will even help determine the criteria by which your work will be evaluated.

❹ What Do You Think?

What do you already know? This unique feature encourages you to explore and discuss the ideas you have on a topic before you begin studying it.

❺ For You to Do

In Active Physics you learn by doing. Activities encourage you to work through problems by yourself, in small groups, or with the whole class.

❻ Physics Talk

When you come across a physics term or equation in the chapter that you may not be familiar with, turn to this feature for a useful, easy-to-understand explanation.

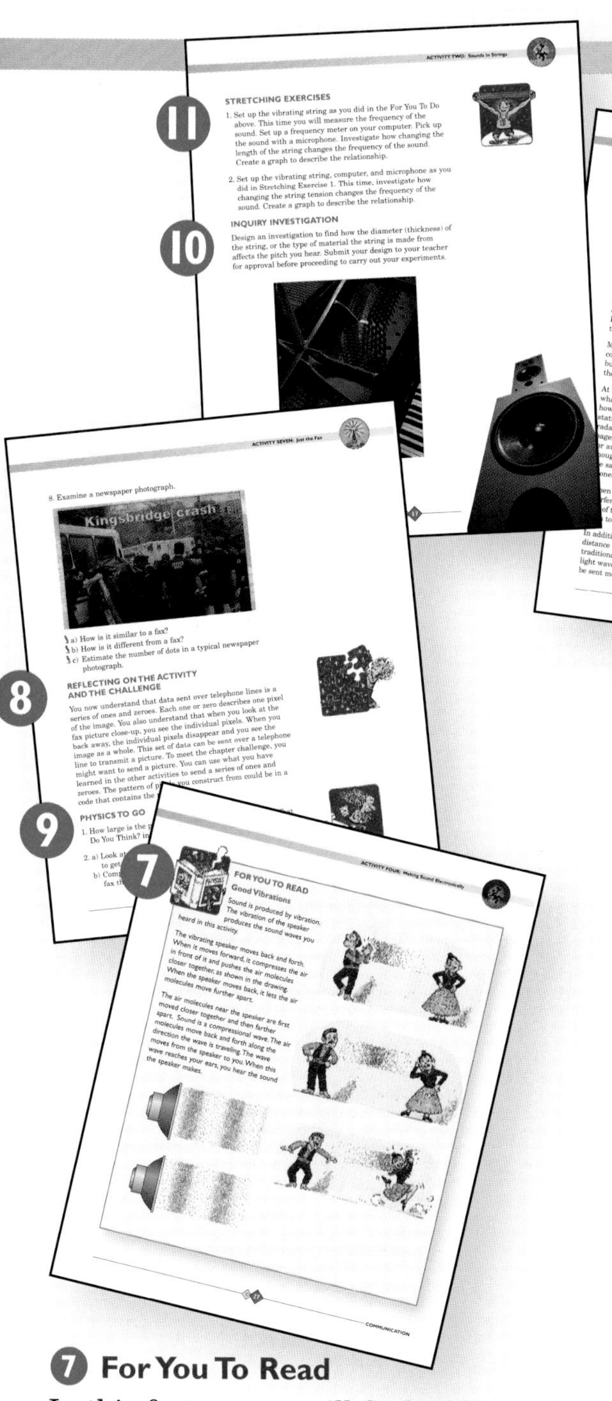

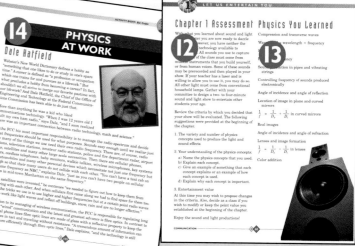

7 For You To Read

In this feature you will find additional insight, or perhaps an interesting new perspective into the topic of the activity.

8 Reflecting on the Activity and the Challenge

Each activity helps prepare you to be successful in the chapter challenge. This feature helps you relate this activity to the larger challenge. It's another piece of the chapter jigsaw puzzle.

9 Physics To Go

Here are exercises, problems, and questions that help you further develop your understanding of the activity and relate it to the chapter challenge.

10 Inquiry Investigation

You are given an opportunity to design your own investigation using the skills you have acquired in the activities.

11 Stretching Exercises

If you're looking for more challenging or in-depth problems, questions, and exercises, you'll find them right here.

12 Chapter Assessment

How do you measure up? Here is your opportunity to share what you have actually learned. Using the activities as a guide, you can now complete the challenge you were presented at the beginning of the chapter.

13 Physics You Learned

This lists the physics terms, principles, and skills you have just learned in the chapter.

14 Physics at Work

Using real people in real jobs, this feature demonstrates how the principles you are learning are being applied everyday, everywhere. It shows that people who use physics can make a difference.

Imagine meeting someone who never heard of your favorite movie or music group! Now imagine how enriched they would be if they could enjoy that movie or music the way you do.

Active Physics came about as a result of a similar frustration. The usual physics course has so much math and so much reading that many students miss the beauty, the excitement, and the usefulness of physics. Many more students simply refuse to take the course. Active Physics began when a group of physicists and physics teachers wondered how to pass on their enjoyment of physics to high school students.

Physics should be experienced and make sense to you. Each chapter of Active Physics begins with a challenge—develop a sport that can be played on the Moon; build a home for people with a housing crisis; pursuade your parents to lend you the family car; and so on. These are tough challenges, but you will learn the physics that will allow you to be successful at every one.

Part of your education is to learn to trust yourself and to question others. When someone tells you something, can they answer your questions: "How do you know? Why should I believe you? and Why should I care?" After Active Physics, when you describe why seatbelts are important, or why loud music can be hazardous, or why communication with extraterrestrials is difficult, and someone asks, "How do you know?" your answer will be, "I know because I did an experiment."

Only a small number of high school students study physics. You are already a part of this select group. Physics awaits your discovery. Enjoy the journey.

Arthur Eisenkraft

Arthur Eisenkraft

CHAPTER
1
LET US ENTERTAIN YOU

Scenario

Most entertainment today comes from the communication of sound and light signals. You look forward to television shows, movies, and rock concerts. The sound signals that entertain you come from voices or musical instruments. Light signals make the images you see on TV or in the movies. Specially designed light patterns add to the effect of a rock concert.

Challenge

You have been made part of a committee to design a two- to four-minute sound and light show to entertain other students your age. But unlike the professionals, you have neither the funds nor the technology available to rock stars or MTV™ productions. All the sounds you use must come from musical instruments or sound makers that you build yourself, or from human voices. Some of these sounds may be prerecorded and then played back during your show. If your teacher has a laser and is willing to allow you to use it, you may do so. All other light must come from conventional household lamps.

Criteria

Work with your classmates to agree on the relative importance of the following assessment criteria. Each item in the list has a point value given after it, but your class must decide what kind of grading system to use.

1. The variety and number of physics concepts used to produce the light and sound effects: (30 points)

   four or more concepts: 30 points

   three concepts: 25 points

   two concepts: 20 points

   one concept: 10 points

2. Your understanding of the physics concepts: (40 points)

   Following your production, you will be asked to:

   a) name the physics concepts that you used. (10 points)
   b) explain each concept. (10 points)
   c) give an example of something that each concept explains or an example of how each concept is used. (10 points)
   d) explain why each concept is important. (10 points)

As a class, you will have to decide if your answers will be in an oral report or a written report.

3. Entertainment value: (30 points)

   Your class will need to decide on a way to assign points for creativity. Note that an entertaining and interesting show need not be loud or bright.

You will have a chance later in the chapter to again discuss these criteria. At that time, you may have more information on the concepts and how you might produce your show. You may want to then propose changes in the criteria and the point values.

Activity One

Making Waves

WHAT DO YOU THINK?

One of the largest tsunamis (tidal waves) grew from about 0.7 m high in the open ocean to 35 m high when it reached shore.

- **How does water move to make a wave?**
- **How does a wave travel?**

Record your ideas about these questions in your *Active Physics log*. Be prepared to discuss your responses with your small group and with your class.

FOR YOU TO DO

1. In an area free of obstacles, stretch out a slinky so the turns are a few centimeters apart. Mark the positions of the end of the slinky by sticking pieces of tape on the floor. Measure the distance between the pieces of tape.

a) Record the distance between the pieces of tape in your log.

2. With the slinky stretched out to the tape, grab the spring near one end, as shown in the drawing, and pull sideways 20 cm and back. To move it correctly, move your wrist like snapping a whip. Observe what happens. You have made a *transverse pulse*.

a) In what direction does the spring move as the pulse goes by?

b) A dictionary definition of transverse is: “Situated or lying across.” Why is transverse a good name for the wave you observed?

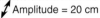

c) Measure and record the amplitude of the wave. The distance you disturbed the spring is called the *amplitude*. The amplitude tells how much the spring is displaced.

3. After you have experimented with making pulses, measure the speed of the pulse. You will need to measure the time it takes the pulse to go the length of the spring. Take several measurements and then average the values.

   a) Record your data in the second and third rows of a table like the one below.

Amplitude	Time for pulse to travel from one end to the other	Average time	Speed = $\frac{\text{length of spring}}{\text{average time}}$

4. Measure the speed of the pulses for two other amplitudes, one larger and one smaller than the value used in step 3.

   a) Record the results in the table in your log.

   b) How does the speed of the pulse depend on the amplitude?

5. Now make waves! Swing one end back-and-forth over and over again along the floor. The result is called a *periodic wave*.

   a) Describe the appearance of the periodic wave you created.

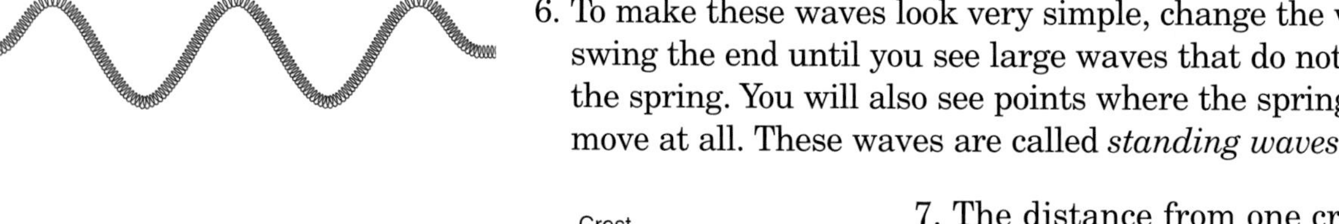

6. To make these waves look very simple, change the way you swing the end until you see large waves that do not move along the spring. You will also see points where the spring does not move at all. These waves are called *standing waves*.

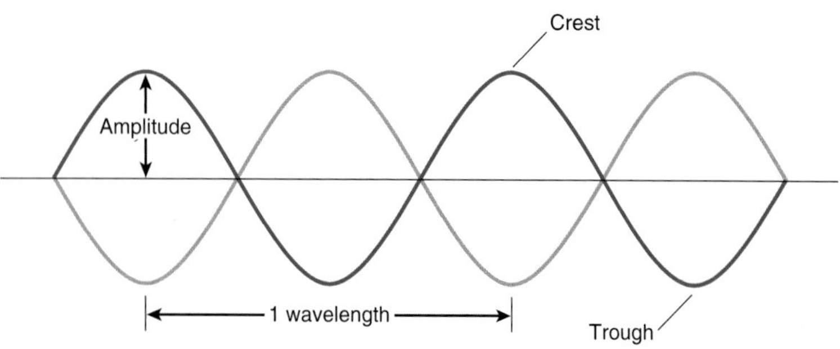

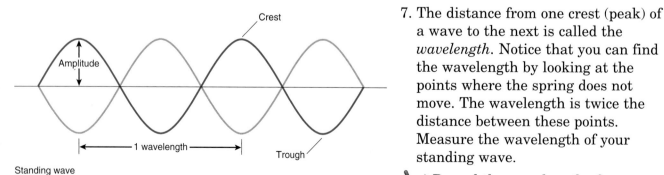

Standing wave

7. The distance from one crest (peak) of a wave to the next is called the *wavelength*. Notice that you can find the wavelength by looking at the points where the spring does not move. The wavelength is twice the distance between these points. Measure the wavelength of your standing wave.

   a) Record the wavelength of your standing wave in your log.

8. You can also measure the wave frequency. The frequency is the number of times the wave moves up and down each second. Measure the frequency of your standing wave. Hint: Watch the hands of the person shaking the spring. Time a certain number of back-and-forth motions. The frequency is the number of back-and-forth motions of the hand in one second.
   a) Record the wave frequency in your log. The unit of frequency is the hertz (Hz).

9. Make several different standing waves by changing the wave frequency. Try to make each standing wave shown in the drawing. Measure the wavelength. Measure the frequency.
   a) Record both in a table like the one below.

Wavelength (m/cycle)	Frequency (cycles/s or Hz)	Speed (m/s) wavelength × frequency

   b) For each wave, calculate the product of the wavelength and the frequency. Compare these values with the average speed of the pulse that you found in steps 3 and 4 above.

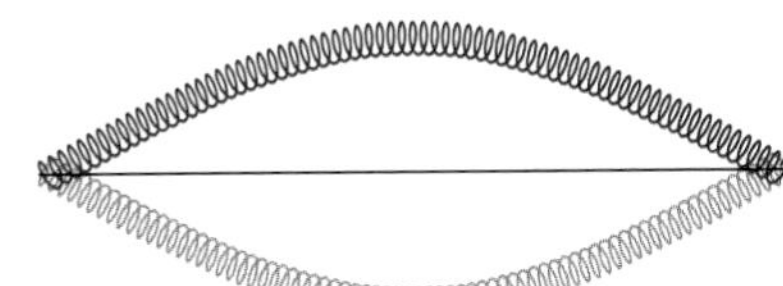

Wavelength = twice slinky length

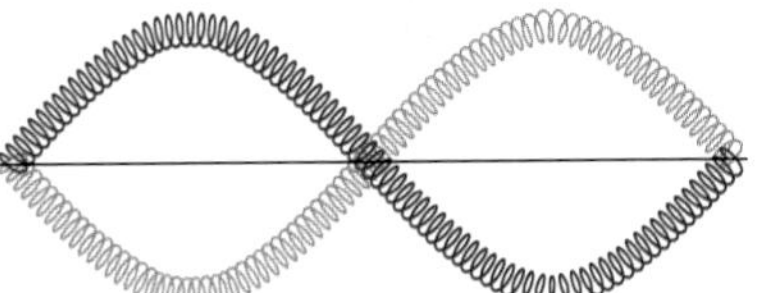

Wavelength = slinky length

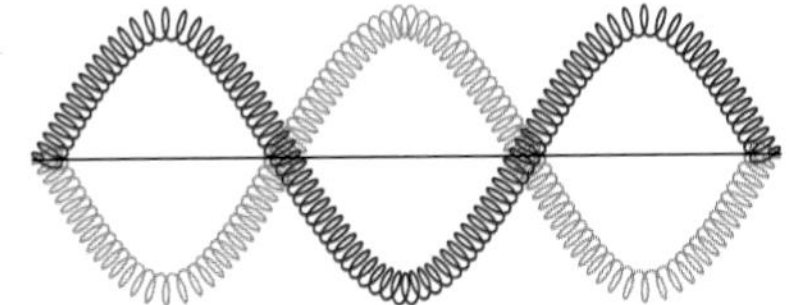

Wavelength = 2/3 slinky length

10. All the waves you have made so far are transverse waves. A different kind of wave is the *compressional* (or *longitudinal*) wave. Have the members of your group stretch out the slinky between the pieces of tape and hold the ends firmly. To make a compressional wave, squeeze together part of the spring and let it go. Measure the speed of the compressional wave and compare it with the speed of the transverse wave.

   a) Record your results in a table partly like the one after step 3.
   b) In what direction does the slinky move as the wave goes by?

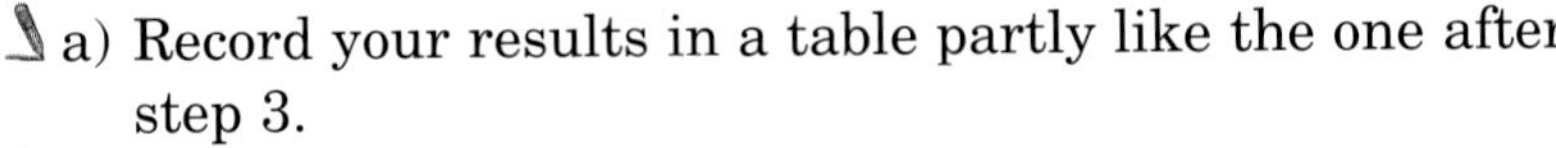

c) A dictionary definition of compressional is: "*a*. The act or process of compressing. *b*. The state of being compressed." A dictionary definition of longitudinal is: "Placed or running lengthwise." Explain why compressional or longitudinal wave is a suitable name for this type of wave.

11. To help you understand waves better, construct a wave viewer by cutting a slit in a file card and labeling it as shown.

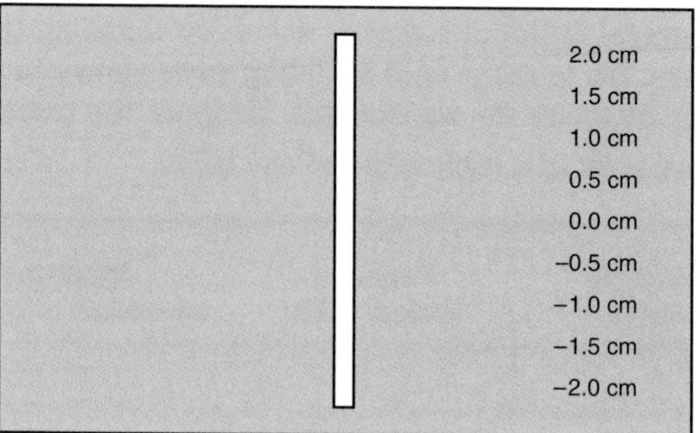

12. Make a drawing of a transverse wave on a strip of adding machine tape. Place this strip under the wave viewer so you can see one part of the wave through the slit.

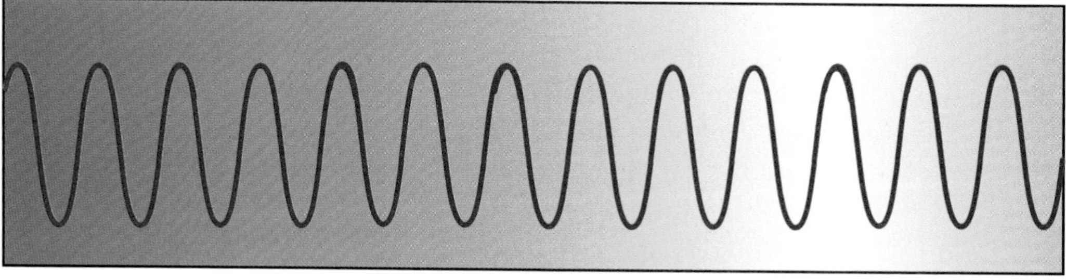

13. With the slit over the tape, pull the tape so that the wave moves. You will see a part of the wave (through the slit) going up and down.

14. Draw waves with different wavelengths on other pieces of adding machine tape. Put these under the slit and pull the adding machine tape at the same speed.

a) Describe what you see.

PHYSICS TALK

Calculating the Speed of Waves

You can find the speed of a wave by measuring the distance the crest moves during a certain change in time.

$$\text{speed} = \frac{\text{change in distance}}{\text{change in time}}$$

In mathematical language:

$$v = \frac{\Delta d}{\Delta t}$$

where v = speed

d = distance

t = time

Suppose the distance the crest moves is 2 m in 0.2 s. The speed can be calculated as follows:

$$v = \frac{\Delta d}{\Delta t} = \frac{2\text{ m}}{0.2\text{ s}} = 10\text{ m/s}$$

The distance from one crest of a wave to the next is the wavelength. The number of crests that go by in one second is the frequency. Imagine you saw five crests go by in one second. You measure the wavelength to be 2 m. The frequency is 5 crests/second, so the speed is $(5 \times 2) = 10$ m/s. Thus the speed can also be found by multiplying the wavelength and the frequency.

$$\text{speed} = \text{frequency} \times \text{wavelength}$$

In mathematical language:

$$v = f\lambda$$

where v = speed

f = frequency

λ = wavelength

REFLECTING ON THE ACTIVITY AND THE CHALLENGE

Slinky waves are easy to observe. You have created transverse and compressional slinky waves, and measured their speed, wavelength, and frequency. For the challenge, you may want to create musical instruments. You will receive more guidance in doing this in the next activities. Your instruments will probably not be made of slinkies. You may, however, use strings that behave just like slinkies. When you have to explain how your instrument works, you can relate its production of sound in terms of the slinky waves that you observed in this activity.

PHYSICS TO GO

1. a) Four characteristics of waves are amplitude, wavelength, frequency, and speed. For each characteristic, tell how you measured it when you worked with the slinky.
   b) For each characteristic, give the units you used in your measurement.
   c) Which wave characteristics are related to each other? Tell how they are related.

2. a) Suppose you shake a long slinky slowly back and forth. Then you shake it rapidly. Describe how the waves change when you shake the slinky more rapidly.
   b) What wave properties change?
   c) What wave properties do not change?

3. Suppose you took a photograph of a wave on a slinky. How can you measure wavelength by looking at the photograph?

4. Suppose you mount a video camera on a tripod and aim the camera at one point on a slinky. You also place a clock next to the slinky, so the video camera records the time. When you look at the video of a wave going by on the slinky, how could you measure the frequency?

5. a) What are the units of wavelength?
   b) What are the units of frequency?
   c) What are the units of speed?
   d) Tell how you find the wave speed from the frequency and the wavelength.
   e) Using your answer to part (d), show how the units of speed are related to the units of wavelength and frequency.

6. a) What is a standing wave?
   b) Draw a standing wave.
   c) Add labels to your drawing to show how the slinky moves.
   d) Tell how to find the wavelength by observing a standing wave.

7. a) Explain the difference between transverse waves and compressional waves.
   b) Slinky waves can be either transverse or compressional. Describe how the slinky moves in each case.

8. a) When you made standing waves, how did you shake the spring (change the frequency) to make the wavelength shorter?
   b) When you made standing waves, how did you shake the spring (change the frequency) to make the wavelength longer?

9. Use the wave viewer and adding machine tape to investigate what happens if the speed of the wave increases. Pull the tape at different speeds and report your results.

Activity Two

Sounds in Strings

WHAT DO YOU THINK?

When the ancient Greeks made stringed musical instruments, they discovered that cutting the length of the string by half or two-thirds produced other pleasing sounds.

- **How do guitarists or violinists today make different sounds?**

Record your ideas about this question in your *Active Physics log*. Be prepared to discuss your responses with your small group and with your class.

FOR YOU TO DO

1. Carefully mount a pulley over one end of a table. Securely clamp one end of a string to the other end of the table.

2. Tie the other end of the string around a mass hanger. Lay the string over the pulley. Place a pencil under the string near the clamp, so the string can vibrate without hitting the table, as shown in the drawing.

3. Hang one 500 g mass on the mass hanger. Pluck the string, listen to the sound, and observe the string vibrate.
   a) Record your observations in your log in a table similar to the following.

Length of vibrating string	Load on mass hanger	Pitch (high, medium, low)

Make sure the area under the hanging mass is clear (no feet, legs). Also monitor the string for fraying.

4. Use a key or some other small metal object. Press this object down on the string right in the middle, to hold the string firmly against the table. Pluck each half of the string.
   a) Record the result in your table.

5. To change the string length, press down with the key at the different places shown in the diagrams on the next page. Pluck each part of the string.
   a) Record the results in your table.

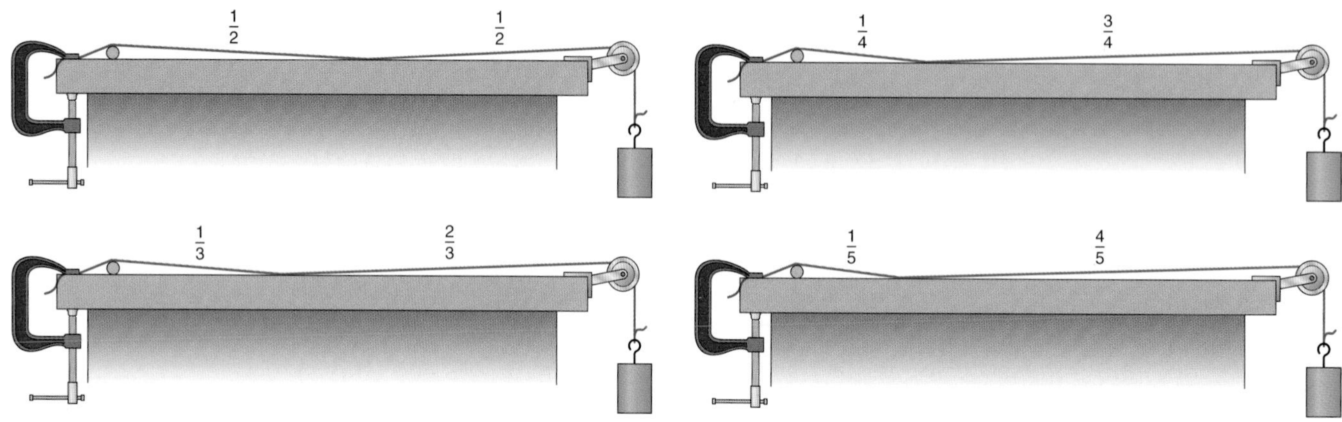

6. When you pluck the string, it does not move at the ends. Look at the drawing on page C7. Measure the length of your string, and find the wavelength of the vibration for each string length.
   a) Record the wavelength in your table.
   b) Look over the data in your table. Make a general statement about what happens to the pitch you hear as you change the length of the string.

Make sure the string is capable of holding 2 kg.

7. Remove the key, so the string is its original length. Pluck the string. To investigate the effect of tightening the string, add a second 500 g mass to the mass hanger. Pluck the string again, observe the vibration, and listen to the pitch of the sound.
   a) Make up a table to record your data in your log.
   b) Add a description of the pitch of the sound to your table. Continue adding weights and observing the sound until the total mass is 2,000 g.
   c) Look over your data. As the mass increases, the string becomes tighter, and its tension increases. Make a general statement about what happens to the pitch you hear as you change the tension on the string.

FOR YOU TO READ

Changing the Pitch

Sound comes from vibration. You observed the vibration of the string as it produced sound. You investigated two of the variables that affect the sound of a vibrating string.

When you pushed the vibrating string down against the table, the length of the string that was vibrating became shorter. Shortening the string increased the pitch (resulted in a higher pitch). In the same way, a guitarist or violinist pushes the string against the instrument to shorten the length that vibrates and increases the pitch.

Also, when you hung weights on the end of the string, that increased the pitch too. These weights tightened the string, so they created more tension in it. As the string tension increased, the pitch of the sound also increased. In tuning a guitar or violin, the performer changes the string tension by turning a peg attached to one end of a string. As the peg pulls the string tighter, the pitch goes up.

Combining these two results into one expression, you can say that increasing the tension or decreasing the length of the string will increase the pitch.

The string producing the pitch is actually setting up a standing wave between its endpoints. The length of the string determines the wavelength of this standing wave. Twice the distance between the endpoints is the wavelength of the sound. The pitch that you hear is related to the frequency of the wave. The higher the pitch, the higher the frequency. The speed of the wave is equal to its frequency multiplied by its wavelength.

$$v = f\lambda$$

where v = speed

f = frequency

λ = wavelength

If the speed of a wave is constant, a decrease in the wavelength will result in an increase in the frequency or a higher pitch. A shortened string produces a higher pitch.

REFLECTING ON THE ACTIVITY AND THE CHALLENGE

Part of the challenge is to create a sound show. In this activity you investigated the relationship of pitch to length of the string and tension of the string: the shorter the string, the higher the pitch; the greater the tension, the higher the pitch. You also learned that the string is setting up a standing wave between its two ends, just like the standing wave that you created in the slinky in Activity One. That's the physics of string instruments! If you wanted to create a string or multi-string instrument for your show, you now know how to adjust the length and tension to produce the notes you want. If you were to make such a stringed instrument, you can explain how you change the pitch by referring to the results of this activity.

PHYSICS TO GO

1. a) Explain how you can change the tension of a vibrating string.
   b) Tell how changing the tension changes the pitch.
2. a) Explain how you can change the length of a vibrating string.
   b) Tell how changing the length changes the sound produced by the string.
3. How would you change both the tension and the length and keep the pitch the same?
4. Suppose you changed both the length and the tension of the string at the same time. What would happen to the sound?
5. a) For the guitar and the piano, tell how the performer plays different notes.
   b) For the guitar and the piano, tell how the performer (or tuner) changes the pitch of the strings to tune the instrument.
6. a) Look at a guitar. Find the tuners (at the end of the neck). Why does a guitar need tuners?
   b) What is the purpose of the frets on a guitar?
   c) Does a violin or a cello have frets?
   d) Why do a violinist and cellist require more accuracy in playing than a guitarist?
7. a) Using what you have learned in this activity, design a simple two-stringed instrument.
   b) Include references to wavelength, frequency, pitch, and standing waves in your description.
   c) Use the vocabulary of wavelength, frequency, and standing waves from Activity One to describe how the instrument works.

STRETCHING EXERCISES

1. Set up the vibrating string as you did in the For You to Do above. This time you will measure the frequency of the sound. Set up a frequency meter on your computer. Pick up the sound with a microphone. Investigate how changing the length of the string changes the frequency of the sound. Create a graph to describe the relationship.

2. Set up the vibrating string, computer, and microphone as you did in Stretching Exercise 1. This time, investigate how changing the string tension changes the frequency of the sound. Create a graph to describe the relationship.

INQUIRY INVESTIGATION

Design an investigation to find how the diameter (thickness) of the string, or the type of material the string is made from affects the pitch you hear. Submit your design to your teacher for approval before proceeding to carry out your experiments.

Activity Three

Sounds from Vibrating Air

WHAT DO YOU THINK?

The longest organ pipes are about 11 m long. A flute, about 0.5 m long, makes musical sound in the same way.

- **How do a flute and organ pipes produce sound?**

Record your ideas about this question in your *Active Physics log*. Be prepared to discuss your responses with your small group and with your class.

FOR YOU TO DO

1. Carefully cut a drinking straw in half. Cut one of the halves into two quarters. Cut one of the quarters into two eighths. Pass one part of the straw out to one member of your group.

2. Gently blow into the top of the piece of straw.
   - a) Describe what you hear.
   - b) Listen as the members of your group blow into their straw pieces one at a time. Describe what you hear.
   - c) Write a general statement about how changing the length of the straw changes the pitch you hear.

3. Now cover the bottom of your straw piece and blow into it again. Uncover the bottom and blow again.
   - a) Compare the sound the straw makes when the bottom is covered and then uncovered.
   - b) Listen as the members of your group blow into their straw pieces, with the bottom covered and then uncovered. Write a general statement about how changing the length of the straw changes the pitch you hear when one end is covered.

4. Obtain a set of four test tubes. Leave one empty. Fill the next halfway with water. Fill the next three-quarters of the way. Fill the last one seven-eighths of the way.

Make sure the outside of the tubes are dry.

5. Give each test tube to one member of your group. Blow across your test tube.
   - a) Describe what you hear.
   - b) Listen as the members of your group blow, one at a time, across their test tubes. Record what you hear.
   - c) What pattern do you find in your observations?
   - d) Compare the results of blowing across the straws with blowing across the test tubes. How are the results consistent?

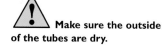

PHYSICS TALK

Vibrating Columns of Air

The sound you heard when you blew into the straw and test tube was produced by a standing wave. If both ends of the straw are open, the air at both ends moves back and forth. The drawing shows the movement of the air as a standing wave.

Tube is open at both ends.
1/2 wavelength fits in straw.

When you covered the other end of the straw, you prevented the air from moving at the covered end. The drawing shows the movement of the air as a standing wave.

Tube is closed at one end.
1/4 wavelength fits in straw.

The velocity of a wave is equal to the frequency multiplied by the wavelength. Therefore,

$$\text{frequency} = \frac{\text{wave speed}}{\text{wavelength}}$$

Using mathematical symbols:

$$f = \frac{v}{\lambda}$$

As the wavelength increases, the frequency decreases. The wavelength in the open straw is half the wavelength in the straw closed at one end. This equation predicts that the frequency of the standing wave in the open straw is twice the frequency of the standing wave in the straw closed at one end.

FOR YOU TO READ

Compressing Air to Make Sound

Sound is a compression wave. The molecules of air bunch up or spread apart as the sound wave passes by.

At the end where the tube is closed, the air cannot go back-and-forth, because its motion is blocked by the end of the tube. That's why the wave's amplitude goes to zero at the closed end. At the open end, the amplitude is as large as it can possibly be. This back-and-forth motion of air at the open end makes a sound wave that moves from the tube to your ear.

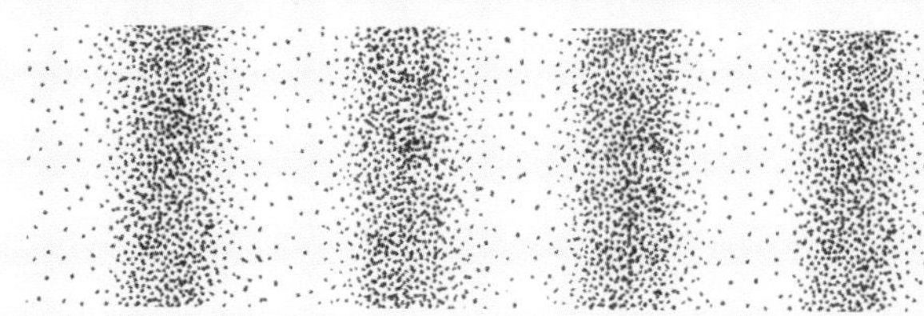

In the compressional slinky wave, the coils of the slinky bunched up in a similar fashion when the slinky wave passed by.

REFLECTING ON THE ACTIVITY AND THE CHALLENGE

In this activity you have observed the sounds produced by different kinds of pipes. If the pipe is cut to a shorter length, the pitch of the sound increases. Also, when the pipe is open at both ends, the pitch is much higher than if the pipe were open at only one end. You have seen how simple drawings of standing waves in these tubes help you find the wavelength of the sound. If the tube is closed at one end, the air has zero displacement at that end. If the tube is open at one end, the air has maximum displacement there.

For your sound show, you may decide to create some "wind" instruments using test tubes or straws, or other materials approved by your teacher. When it comes time to explain how these work, you can refer to this activity to get the physics right.

PHYSICS TO GO

1. a) You can produce a sound by plucking a string or by blowing in a pipe. How are these two ways of producing sound similar?

   b) How are these two ways different?

2. a) For each piece of straw your group used, make a full-sized drawing to show the standing wave inside. Show both the straw closed at one end and open at both ends.

   b) Next to each drawing of the standing waves, make a drawing, at the same scale, of one full wavelength. You may need to tape together several pieces of paper for this drawing.

   c) Frequency times the wavelength is the wave speed. The speed is the same for all frequencies. From your answer to part (b), what can you predict about the frequencies of the standing waves in the straw pieces?

   d) How well do your predictions from part (c) agree with your observations in this activity?

3. a) What is the length, in meters, of the longest organ pipe?

   b) Assume this pipe is closed at one end. Draw the standing wave pattern.

   c) For this pipe, how long is the wavelength of this standing wave?

   d) Why does a long wavelength indicate that the frequency will be low? Give a reason for your answer.

4. a) Suppose you are listening to the sound of an organ pipe that is closed at one end. The pipe is 3 m long. What is the wavelength of the sound in the pipe?

   b) The speed of sound in air is about 340 m/s. What is the frequency of the sound wave?

   c) Now suppose you are listening to the sound of an organ pipe that is open at both ends. As before, the pipe is 3 m long. What is the wavelength of the sound in the pipe?

   d) What is the frequency of the sound wave?

5. Suppose you listen to the sound of an organ pipe that is closed at one end. This pipe is only 1 m long. How does its frequency compare with the frequency you found in question 4, part (b)?

STRETCHING EXERCISES

1. If you have a good musical ear, add water to eight test tubes to make a scale. Play a simple piece for the class.

2. Obtain a two-to-three meter long piece of a seven- to ten-centimeter diameter plastic pipe, like that used to filter water in small swimming pools. In an area free of obstructions, twirl the pipe overhead. What can you say about how the sound is formed? Place some small bits of paper on a stool. Twirl the pipe and keep one end right over the stool. What happens to the paper? What does that tell you about the air flowing through the pipe? Try to play a simple tune by changing the speed of the pipe as you twirl it.

3. Carefully cut new straw pieces, as you did in For You To Do, step 1 above. This time you will measure the frequency of the sound. Set up a frequency meter on your computer. Place the microphone near an open end of the straw. As before, each person blows into only one piece of straw. Make the sound and record the frequency. Now cover the end of the straw and predict what frequency you will measure. Make the measurement and compare it with your prediction. Repeat the measurements for all four lengths of straw. Record your results, and tell what patterns you find.

Activity Four

Making Sound Electronically

WHAT DO YOU THINK?

You have seen products, like greeting cards or toys, that produce sound.

- **How is sound produced by these "instruments?"**
- **How expensive and complex could it be to produce sounds this way?**

Record your ideas about these questions in your *Active Physics log*. Be prepared to discuss your responses with your small group and with your class.

FOR YOU TO DO

1. Obtain the equipment shown in the diagram from your teacher. Use the diagram to identify each piece.

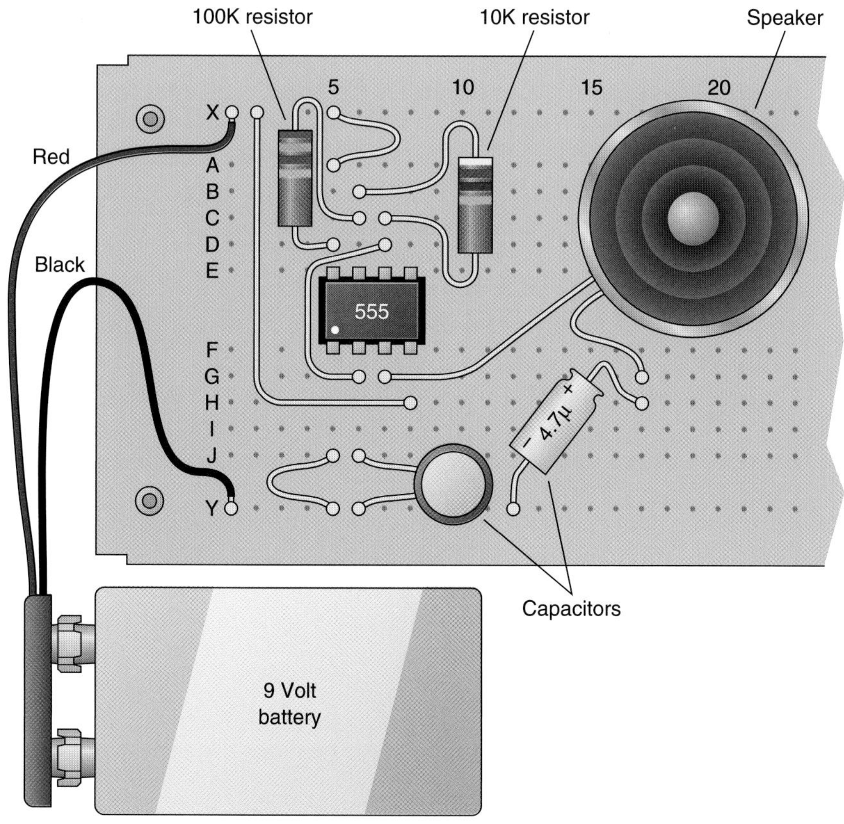

2. Find the socket board and turn it as shown in the drawing. Look at the diagram. See how each row (across) and each column (up and down) are labeled. Notice that the 555 timer is already shown installed on the board.
   a) In your log, make a drawing of the 555 timer as it is shown above. On your drawing, label the coordinates of each of the corner pins.

3. Find the four connection wires. Be sure that about 1 cm of insulation has been removed from each end. Connect them as follows:
   - Connect one wire from X5 TO A5.
   - Connect one wire from J5 to Y5.
   - Connect one wire from D7 to G6.
   - Connect one wire from X2 to H8.

   When you have finished, compare your wiring with the drawing.

4. The resistors are small cylinders with colored bands. You can connect them in either direction. Find the resistor with brown, black, and yellow bands. Connect this resistor to D5 and C6.

5. Find the resistor with brown, black, and orange bands. Connect this resistor to B6 and C7.

6. Find the capacitor that says 4.7 μ and has a "+" sign at one end and a "−" sign at the other. A capacitor is a small cylinder with two wires coming out of the edge of the disk. Connect the "+" wire to H17. Connect the "−" wire to Y12.

7. Find the other capacitors. These capacitors are disks. Connect one of these capacitors to J6 and Y6.

8. Connect the speaker to G7 and G17.

9. Connect the red wire of the battery clip to X1 and the black wire to Y1.

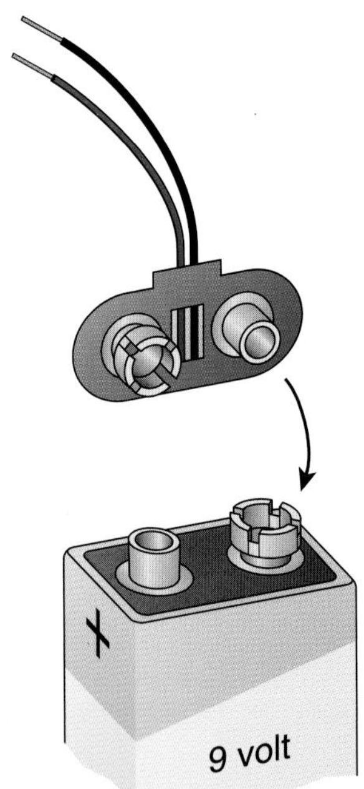

10. Look at the battery and battery clip. Compare what you see with the drawing. Snap the clip onto the battery, as shown. Observe what happens.
    a) Record in your log what happens.

11. Return to the circuit board and do the following:
    a) Go back to the capacitor that you connected to J6 and Y6. Replace this with one of the other capacitors. What happens?
    b) Replace it with the third capacitor. What happens?
    c) Switch the two resistors. What happens?
    d) How do you think the sound wave changed when you changed capacitors or resistors? What did you hear?

12. Make the pitch of the sound as low as you can.
    a) Which capacitor are you using? Where are the resistors?
    b) Gently touch the speaker cardboard while the tone is sounding. What do you feel?

FOR YOU TO READ

Good Vibrations

Sound is produced by vibration. The vibration of the speaker produces the sound waves you heard in this activity.

The vibrating speaker moves back and forth. When it moves forward, it compresses the air in front of it and pushes the air molecules closer together, as shown in the drawing. When the speaker moves back, it lets the air molecules move further apart.

The air molecules near the speaker are first moved closer together and then farther apart. Sound is a compressional wave. The air molecules move back and forth along the direction the wave is traveling. The wave moves from the speaker to you. When this wave reaches your ears, you hear the sound the speaker makes.

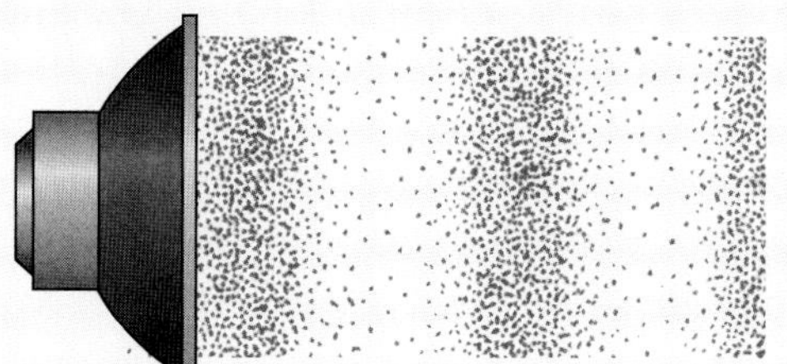

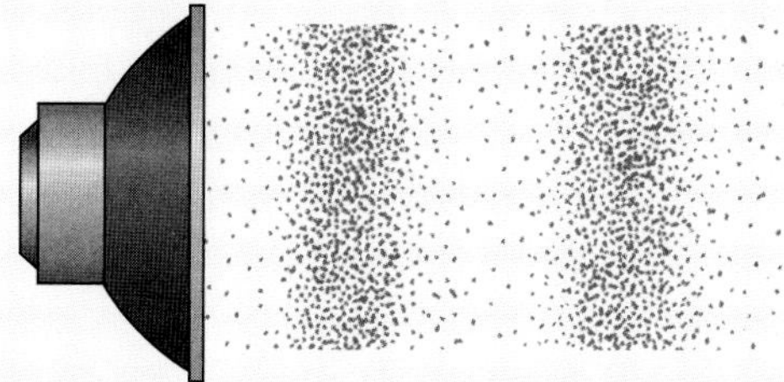

REFLECTING ON THE ACTIVITY AND THE CHALLENGE

In this activity you have learned how to build a simple circuit that produces sounds. You have discovered that by changing the parts, you can control the pitch of the sound. You felt the vibrations in the material of the speaker that produces the sound. With what you have learned about sound, you know that a different pitch means a different frequency. So you have made a device that could be part of a musical instrument, since you can make sounds and control the pitch of the sound. Perhaps you can use this electronics technology in your sound and light show. You might build a circuit with several capacitors connected to push buttons, so the audience could play different notes by pushing these buttons.

PHYSICS TO GO

1. a) How did you change your circuit to change the pitch of the sound?
   b) Describe the changes that increased the pitch.
   c) Describe the changes that decreased the pitch.

2. a) In a rock concert, what do you feel in your chest when the bass is playing its lowest notes?
   b) How does that compare to what you felt when you touched the speaker in the above activity?

3. The illustration shows a circuit diagram of the circuit you built. This drawing shows the wires and connections in a special way. Show that the diagram describes the circuit you built.

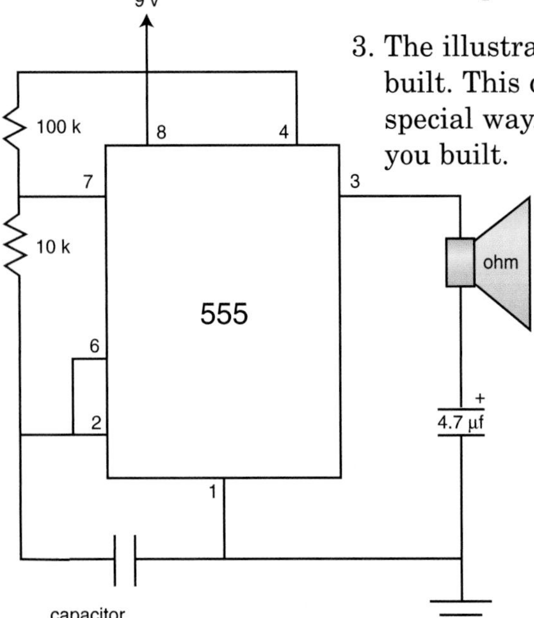

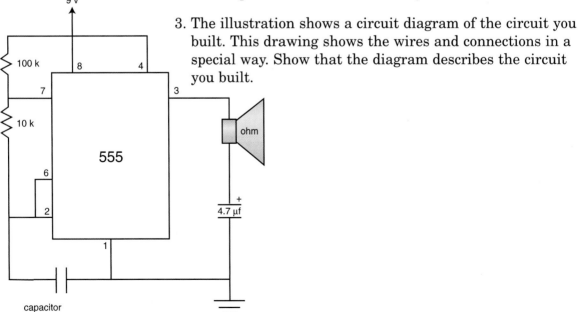

4. Invent and describe a way in which to replace the capacitors very quickly so that notes can be played in succession.

5. Create a design for an electronic piano where each key produces a different note. Make a list of the materials you will need for this piano. What would be the price you would expect that someone may spend for such an instrument?

STRETCHING EXERCISES

1. Work with other groups of students to make a musical instrument out of the circuits that you make in this activity. Find a way to tune each group's circuit so that each one plays a musical note. Perform a tune for the class.

2. Use an oscilloscope to observe the signal that your circuit sends to the speaker. Report your findings to the class.

3. Set up a continuity tester by wiring up a light bulb and a battery. Use your tester to find out which sockets in your socket board are connected together. Make a drawing of the board to show the connections.

Activity Five

Reflected Light

WHAT DO YOU THINK?

Astronauts placed a mirror on the moon in 1969 so that a light beam sent from Earth could be reflected back to Earth. By timing the return of the beam, scientists found the distance between the Earth and the moon. They measured this distance to within 30 cm.

- **How are you able to see yourself in a mirror?**
- **If you want to see more of yourself, what can you do?**

Record your ideas about these questions in your *Active Physics log*. Be prepared to discuss your responses with your small group and with your class.

FOR YOU TO DO

1. Place a piece of paper on your desk. Carefully aim the laser pointer, or the light from a ray box, so the light beam moves horizontally, as shown.

2. Place a glass rod in the light beam so that the beam spreads up-and-down. Shine the beam on the piece of paper to be sure the beam passed through the glass rod.

3. Carefully stand the plane mirror on your desk in the middle of the piece of paper. Draw a line on the paper along the front edge of the mirror. Now remove the mirror and draw a dotted line perpendicular to the first line, as shown. This dotted line is called the normal.

Do not use mirrors with chipped edges. Make sure the ends of the glass rod are polished.

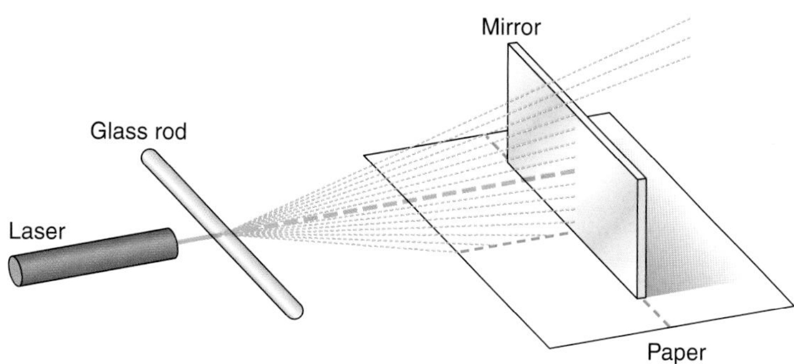

4. Aim the light source so the beam approaches the mirror along the normal. Be sure the glass rod is in place to spread out the beam.
   a) What happens to the light after it hits the mirror?

Never look directly at a laser beam or shine a laser beam into someone's eyes. Always work above the plane of the beam and beware of reflections from shiny surfaces.

5. Make the light hit the mirror at a different angle.
   a) What happens now?
   b) On the paper, mark three or more dots under the beam to show the direction of the beam as it travels to the mirror. The line you traced shows the *incident ray*. Also make dots to show the light going away from the mirror. This line shows the *reflected ray*. Label this pair of rays to show they go together.

6. Turn the light source so it starts from the same point but strikes the mirror at different angles. For each angle, mark dots on the paper to show the direction of the incident and reflected rays. Also, label each pair of rays.

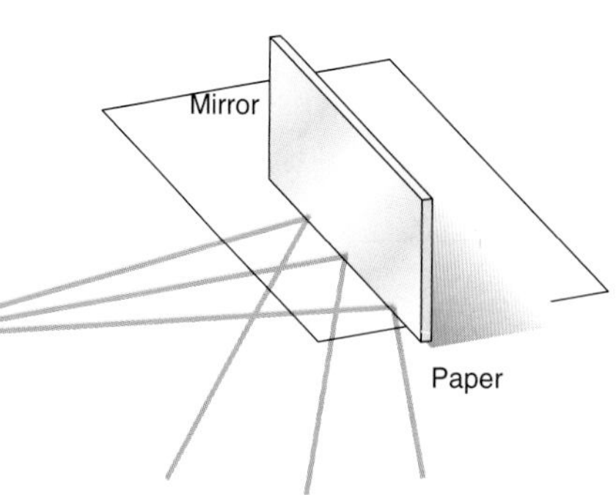

7. Most lab mirrors have the reflecting surface on the back. In addition, the light bends as it enters and leaves the glass part of the mirror. In your drawing, the rays may not meet at the mirror surface. Extend the rays until they do meet.
   a) Measure these angles for one pair of your rays.

8. Turn off the light source and remove the paper. Look at one pair of rays. The diagram shows a top view of the mirror, the normal, and an incident and reflected ray. Notice the angle of incidence and the angle of reflection in the drawing. Using a protractor, measure these angles for one pair of rays.
   a) Record your data in a table.
   b) Measure and record the angles of incidence and reflection for all of your pairs of rays.

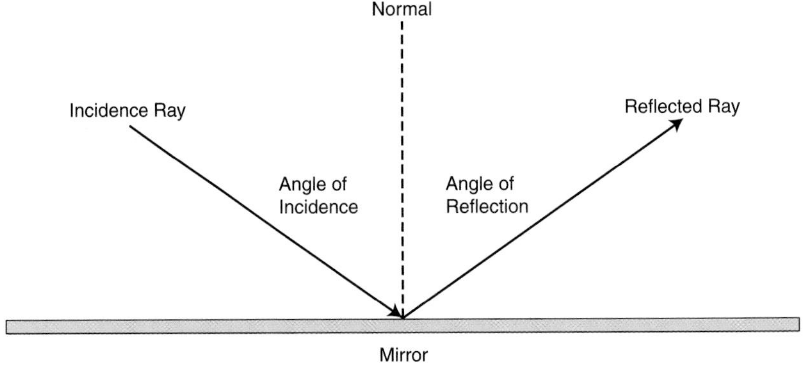

   c) What is the relationship between the angles of incidence and reflection?
   d) Look at the reflected rays in your drawing. Extend each ray back behind the mirror. What do you notice when you have extended all the rays? The position where the rays meet is the location of the *image* of the light source. All of the light rays leave one point in front of the mirror. The reflected rays all seem to emerge from one point behind the mirror. Wherever you observed the reflection, you would see the source at this point behind the mirror.
   e) Tape a copy of your diagram in your log.

9. Hold the light source, or any object, near the mirror and look at the reflection. Now hold the object far away and again look at the reflection.
   a) How is the position of the reflection related to the position of the object?

10. Set up a mirror on another piece of paper, and draw the normal on the paper. Write your name in block capital letters along the normal (a line perpendicular to the mirror). Observe the reflection of your name in the mirror.
   a) How can you explain the reflection you see?
   b) Which letters in the reflection are closest to the mirror? Which are farthest away?
   c) In your log, make a sketch of your name and its reflection.

11. Carefully stand up two mirrors so they meet at a right angle. Be sure they touch each other, as shown in the drawing.

12. Place an object in front of the mirrors.
   a) How many images do you see?
   b) Slowly change the angle between the mirrors. Make a general statement about how the number of images you see changes as the angle between the mirrors changes.

FOR YOU TO READ

Images in a Plane Mirror

An object like the tip of a nose reflects light in all directions. That is why everybody in a room can see the tip of a nose. Light reflects off a mirror in such a way that the angle of incidence is equal to the angle of reflection. You can look at the light leaving the tip of a nose and hitting a mirror to see how an image is produced and where it is located. Each ray of light leaves the nose at a different angle. Once it hits the mirror, the angle of incidence must equal the angle of reflection. There are now a set of rays diverging from the mirror. If you assume that the light always traveled in straight lines, you can extend these rays behind the mirror and find where they "seem" to emerge from. That is the location of the image.

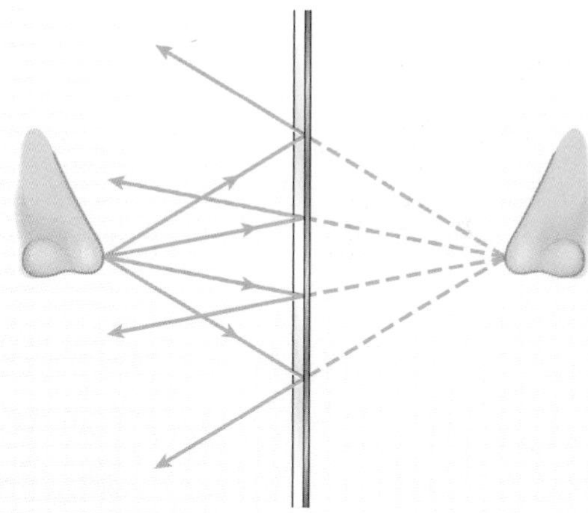

The mirror does such a good job in reflecting that it looks as if there is a tip of a nose (and all other parts of the face) behind the mirror. If you measure the distance of the image behind the mirror, you will find that it is equal to the distance of the nose (object) in front of the mirror. This can also be proven using geometry.

REFLECTING ON THE ACTIVITY AND THE CHALLENGE

In this activity you aimed light rays at mirrors and observed the reflections. From the experiment you discovered that the angle of incidence is equal to the angle of reflection. Therefore, you can now predict the path of a reflected light beam. You also experimented with reflections from two mirrors. When you observed the reflection in two mirrors, you found many images which made interesting patterns.

This activity has given you experience with many interesting effects that you can use in your sound and light show. For instance, you may want to show the audience a reflection in one mirror or two mirrors placed at angles. You can probably create a kaleidoscope. You will also be able to explain the physics concept you use in terms of reflected light.

PHYSICS TO GO

1. How is the way light reflects from a mirror similar to the way a tennis ball bounces off a wall?

2. a) What is the normal to a plane mirror?
   b) When a light beam reflects from a plane mirror, how do you measure the angle of incidence?
   c) How do you measure the angle of reflection?
   d) What is the relationship between the angle of incidence and the angle of reflection?

3. Make a top-view drawing to show the relationships among the normal, the angle of incidence, and the angle of reflection.

4. a) Suppose you are experimenting with a mirror mounted vertically on a table, like the one you used in this activity. Make a top-view drawing, with a heavy line to represent the mirror and a dotted line to represent the normal.
   b) Show light beams that make angles of incidence of 0°, 30°, 45°, and 60° to the normal.
   c) For each of the above beams, draw the reflected ray. Add a label if necessary to show where the rays are.

5. a) Stand in front of a mirror.
   b) Move your hand towards the mirror. Which way does the reflection move?
   c) Move your hand away from the mirror. Which way does the reflection move?
   d) Use what you learned about the position of the mirror image to explain your answers to parts (b) and (c).

6. Suppose you wrote the whole alphabet along the normal to a mirror in the way you wrote your name in step 10.
   a) Which letters would look just like their reflections?
   b) Write three words that would look just like their reflections.
   c) Write three letters that would look different from their reflections.
   d) Draw the reflection of each letter you gave in part (c).

7. Why is the word "Ambulance" written in an unusual way on the front of an ambulance?

STRETCHING EXERCISES

1. Carefully tape together three small mirrors to make a corner reflector. Shine a flashlight down into the corner. Where does the reflected beam go?

2. Build a kaleidoscope by **carefully** inserting two mirrors inside a paper towel holder. Also, you can use three identical mirrors. Do not force the mirrors into the tube. Tape the edges of the mirrors together, with the mirrored surfaces inside. Describe what you see through your kaleidoscope.

3. Carefully tape together one edge of two mirrors so they can move like a hinge, with the mirrored surfaces facing each other. Place a small object between the mirrors. Investigate how the number of images you see depends on the angle between the mirrors. You will need a protractor to measure this angle. Plot a graph of the results. What mathematical relationship can you find between the angle and the number of images?

Activity Six

Curved Mirrors

WHAT DO YOU THINK?

The curved mirror of the Palomar telescope is five meters across. Mirrors with varying curvatures are used in amusement parks as fun-house mirrors. Store mirrors and car, side-view mirrors are also curved.

- **How is what you see in curved mirrors different from ordinary flat mirrors?**

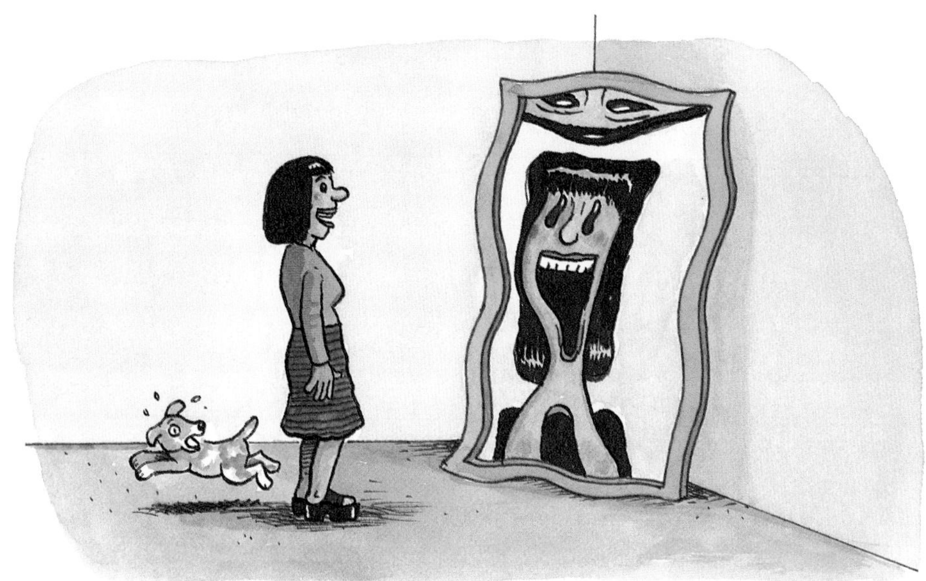

Record your ideas about this question in your *Active Physics log*. Be prepared to discuss your responses with your small group and with your class.

FOR YOU TO DO

1. Carefully aim a laser pointer, or the light from a ray box, so the light beam moves horizontally, as you did in Activity Five. Place a glass rod in the light beam so that the beam spreads up-and-down. See the diagram on page C31.

2. Fasten a strip of mylar sheet to the outside of a gently curved piece of Styrofoam® or cardboard to make a *convex* surface. Place the mirror in the light beam, as shown in the drawing.

3. Shine a beam directly at the center of the mirror. This is the *incident* beam. Show its path by placing three or more dots on the paper, as you did in Activity Five. Connect the dots to make a straight line. Find the reflected ray and mark its path in a similar way. Label the two lines so you will know they go together.

Never look directly at a laser beam or shine a laser beam into someone's eyes. Always work above the plane of the beam and beware of reflections from shiny surfaces.

4. You will move the light source sideways to make a series of parallel beams. To make sure the incident beams are parallel, line up each one with the dots you made to show the incoming beam in step 3. Mark the path of the incoming ray with three dots.

5. Each parallel beam makes a reflected beam. Show the path of each of these reflected rays. Label each incident and reflected beam so you will know that they go together.
   a) Write a sentence to tell what happens to the parallel beams after they are reflected.
   b) Make a drawing in your *Active Physics log* to record the path of the light.

6. Remove the mirror. With a ruler, extend each reflected ray backwards to the part of the paper that was behind the mirror.
   a) You probably noticed that all the lines converge in a single point. The place where the extended rays meet is called the *focus* of the mirror. The distance from this point to the mirror is called the *focal length.* Measure and record this focal length.

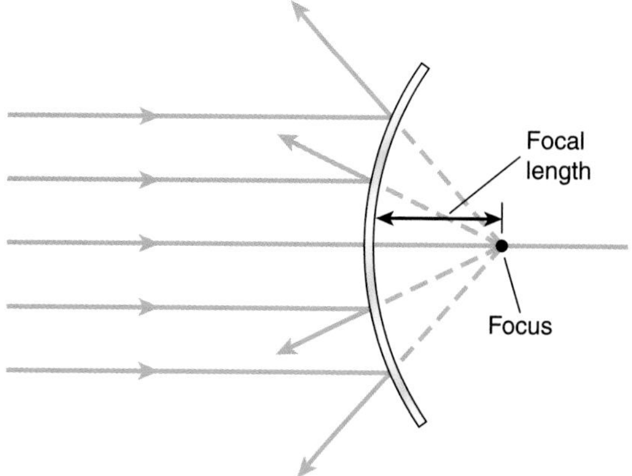

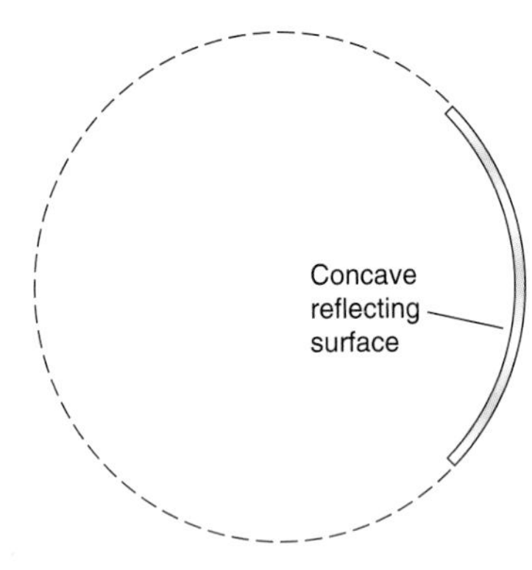

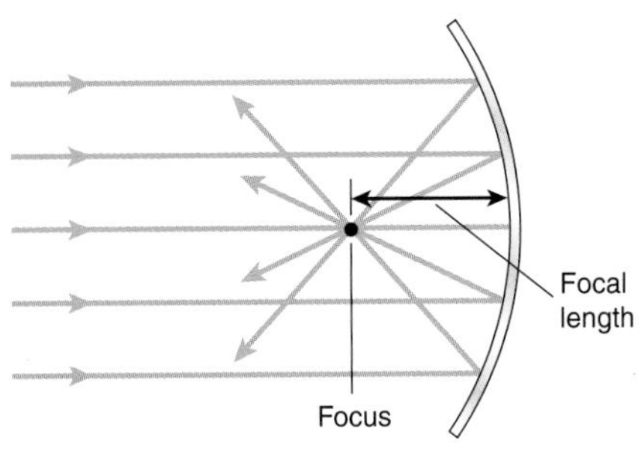

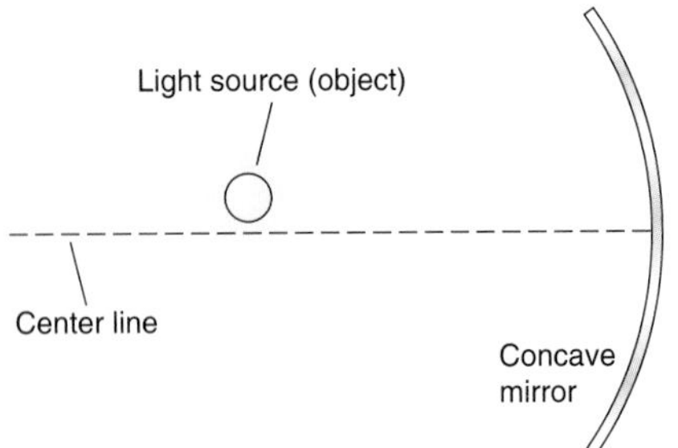

7. Remove the Mylar sheet from the outside of the curved surface and fasten it on the inside of the curved form, as shown. You have made a *concave* surface. To help you remember this name, think of the concave mirror as "caving in." Repeat steps 3 through 5 for this mirror.

   a) Write a sentence to tell what happens to the parallel beams after they are reflected from the concave mirror.

   b) Make a drawing in your *Active Physics log* to record the path of the light. The place where the beams cross is called the focus. The distance from the focus to the mirror is the focal length.

   c) Measure and record the focal length.

   d) How do concave and convex mirrors reflect light differently? Record your answer in your log.

8. Use a concave mirror that your teacher has supplied. Use a 40-W light bulb or a candle as a light source, which will be called the "object." Carefully mount your mirror so it is at the same height as the light source. Place a light bulb about a meter away from the mirror. Put the bulb slightly off the center line, as shown, so that an index card will not block the light from hitting the mirror.

9. Try to find the image of the object on an index card. Move the card back and forth until the image is sharp. The image you found is called a *real* image because you are able to project it on a card.

   a) Record the distance of the bulb from the mirror and the image on the file card from the mirror. Put your results in the first line of a table like the one below.

Distance of bulb from mirror	Distance of image from mirror

10. Carefully move the mirror closer to the object. Find the sharp image, as before, by moving the index card back and forth.
    a) Record the image and object distances in your table.
    b) Repeat the measurement for at least six object locations.
    c) Draw a graph of the image distance (y-axis) versus the object distance (x-axis).
    d) Write a sentence that describes the relationship between the image distance and the object distance.

11. A mathematical relation that describes concave mirrors is

$$\frac{1}{f} = \frac{1}{D_o} + \frac{1}{D_i}$$

where f is the focal length of that particular mirror,

D_o is the object distance

D_i is the image distance

You have measured D_o and D_i. Calculate $\frac{1}{D_o}$ and $\frac{1}{D_i}$. Find their sum for each pair of data.

    a) Record your calculations in your log.
    b) Are your sums approximately equal? If so, you have mathematically found the value of $\frac{1}{f}$ for the mirror you used.

12. A convex mirror cannot form a real image that can be projected onto a screen. It can form an image behind the mirror, like the plane mirror of Activity Five.
    a) Record in your log descriptions of the image in a convex mirror when the mirror is held close and when the mirror is held far from the object.

PHYSICS TALK

Making Real Images

To find how a concave mirror makes a real image, you can view a few rays of light. Each ray of light obeys the relation you found for plane mirrors (angle of incidence = angle of reflection). In this case, you choose two easily drawn rays.

Look at the drawing. It shows rays coming into a concave mirror from a point on a light bulb. One ray comes in parallel to the dotted line, which is the axis of the mirror. This ray reflects through the focus. The other ray hits the center of the mirror. This ray reflects and makes the same angle with the mirror axis going out as it did coming in. Where these rays meet is the image of the top of the light bulb.

The next drawing shows the same mirror, but with the object much further from the mirror. Notice how the image in this second drawing is much smaller and much closer to the focus.

As you have seen, the position of the object and image are described by the equation below.

$$\frac{1}{f} = \frac{1}{D_o} + \frac{1}{D_i}$$

Look at the graph of this equation. Notice that as the object distance decreases, the image distance becomes very large. As the object distance increases, the image distance moves towards the focal length (f). Also, notice that neither the object distance nor the image distance can be less than the focal length.

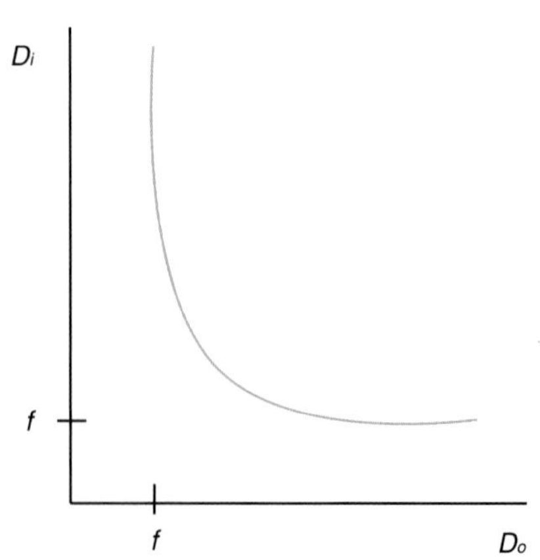

REFLECTING ON THE ACTIVITY AND THE CHALLENGE

You have observed how rays of light are reflected by a curved mirror. You have seen that a concave mirror can make an upside-down, real image (an image on a screen). You have also seen that the image and object distances are described by a simple mathematical relationship. You have also seen that there is no real image in a convex mirror, and the image is always smaller than the object.

You may want to use a curved mirror in your sound and light show. You may want to project an image on a screen or produce a reflection that the audience can see in the mirror. What you have learned will help you explain how these images are made.

Since the image changes with distance, you may try to find a way to have a moving object so that the image will automatically move and change size. A ball suspended by a string in front of a mirror may produce an interesting effect. You may also wish to combine convex and concave mirrors so that some parts of the object are larger and others are smaller. Mylar could be shaped to make some kind of fun-house mirror.

Remember that your light show will be partially judged by creativity and part will be judged by the application of physics principles. This activity has provided you with some useful principles that can help with both criteria.

PHYSICS TO GO

1. a) Make a drawing of parallel laser beams aimed at a convex mirror.
   b) Draw lines to show how the beams reflect from the mirror.

2. a) Make a drawing of parallel laser beams aimed at a concave mirror.
   b) Draw lines to show how the beams reflect from the mirror.

3. a) Look at the back of the spoon. What do you see?
   b) Look at the inside of the spoon. What do you see?

4. a) If you were designing a shaving mirror, would you make it concave or convex? Explain your answer.
   b) Why do some make-up mirrors have two sides? What do the different sides do? How does each side produce its own special view?
   c) How does a curved side mirror on a car produce a useful view? How can this view sometimes be dangerous?
   d) Why does a dentist use a curved mirror?

5. a) A student found the real image of a light bulb in a concave mirror. The student moved the light bulb to different positions. At each position, the student measured the position of the image and the light bulb. The results are shown in the table on the left. Draw a graph of this data.
   b) Make a general statement to summarize how the image distance changes as the object distance changes.
   c) If the object were twice as far away as the greatest object distance in the data, estimate where the image would be.
   d) If the object were only half as far from the mirror as the smallest object distance in the data, estimate what would happen to the image.

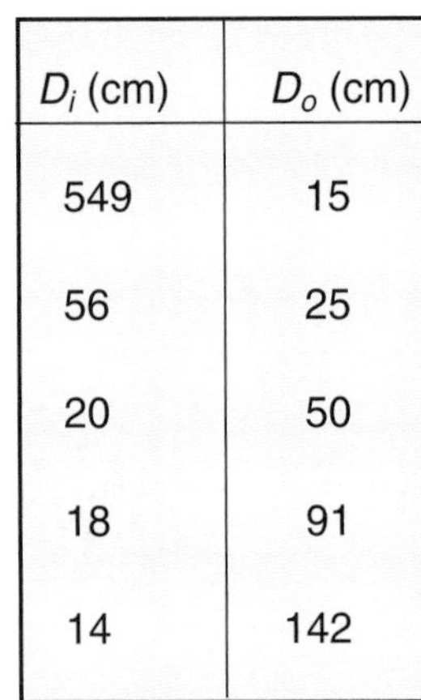

D_i (cm)	D_o (cm)
549	15
56	25
20	50
18	91
14	142

6. A ball is hung on a string in front of a flat mirror. The ball swings toward the mirror and back. How would the image of the ball in the mirror change as the ball swings back and forth?

7. a) If a ball is hung on a string in front of a concave mirror. The ball swings toward the mirror and back. How would the image of the ball in the mirror change as the ball swings back and forth?
   b) How could you use this swinging ball in your light show?

8. Outdoors at night, you use a large concave mirror to make an image on a card of distant auto head lamps. You make the image on a card. What happens to the image as the car gradually comes closer?

Activity Seven

Refraction of Light

WHAT DO YOU THINK?

The Hope Diamond is valued at about 100 million dollars. A piece of cut glass of about the same size is worth only a few dollars.

- **How can a jeweler tell the difference between diamond and cut glass?**

Record your ideas about this question in your *Active Physics log*. Be prepared to discuss your responses with your small group and with your class.

FOR YOU TO DO

1. Place a BLOX (a block of unflavored gelatin) on a piece of waxed paper. Mark the paper around the base of the BLOX and cut out this rectangular piece of waxed paper. Place the rectangular piece of waxed paper on a piece of white paper on your desk. Now place the BLOX on top of the waxed paper.

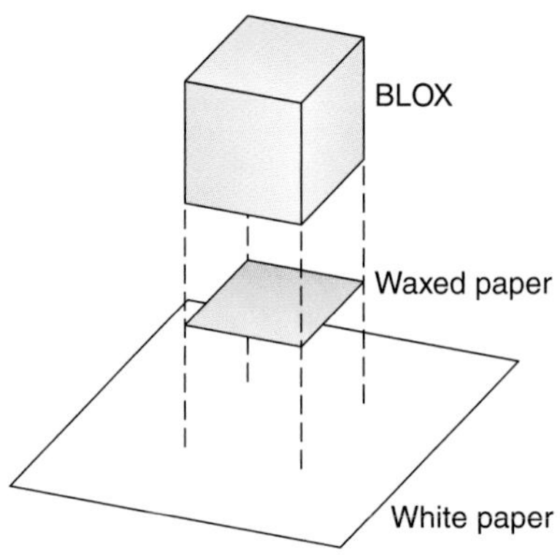

Never look directly at a laser beam or shine a laser beam into someone's eyes. Always work above the plane of the beam and beware of reflections from shiny surfaces.

2. Carefully aim a laser pointer, or the light from a ray box, so the light beam moves horizontally, as you did in Activity Five. Place a glass rod in the light beam so that the beam spreads up-and-down. See the diagram on page C31.

3. Shine the laser pointer or light from the ray box through the BLOX. Be sure the beam leaves the BLOX on the side opposite the side the beam enters. Mark the path of each beam. You may wish to use a series of dots as you did in Activity Five. Label each path on both sides of the BLOX so you will know that they go together.

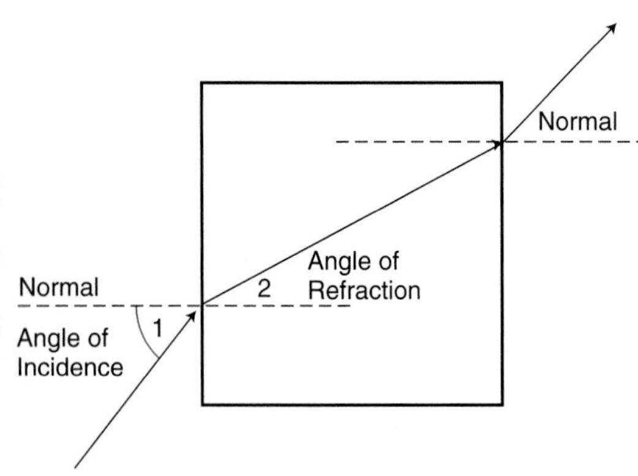

4. The angle of incidence is the angle between the incident laser beam and the normal, as shown in the diagram. Choose two other angles of incidence and again mark the path of the light, as you did in Step 3. As before, label each pair of paths.

5. Trace the outline of the BLOX on the paper, and remove the BLOX. Connect the paths you traced to show the light beam entering the BLOX, traveling through the BLOX and emerging from the BLOX. Draw a perpendicular line at the point where a ray enters or leaves the BLOX. Label this line the normal.

6. Measure the angles of incidence (the angle in the air) and refraction (the angle in the BLOX).

a) Record your measurements in tables like the one shown.

Angle of incidence	Angle of refraction	Sine of angle of incidence	Sine of angle of refraction	$\frac{\text{Sin } \angle i}{\text{Sin } \angle R}$

b) Use a calculator to complete the chart by finding the sines of the angles (sin button on calculator).

c) Is the value of $\frac{\sin \angle i}{\sin \angle R}$ a constant? This value is called the index of refraction for the BLOX.

7. Set up the BLOX on a clean sheet of white paper. This time, as shown in the drawing, aim the beam so it leaves the BLOX on the side, rather than at the back.

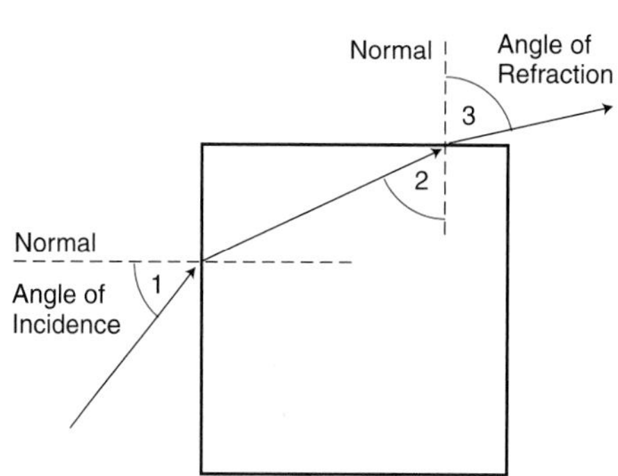

8. Make the first angle of incidence (angle 1) as small as possible, so the second angle of incidence (angle 2) will be as large as possible. Adjust angle 1 so that the beam leaves the BLOX parallel to the side of the BLOX, as shown. Measure the value of angle 2.

a) Record the value of angle 2. It is called the *critical* angle.

b) What happens to the beam if you make angle 2 greater than the critical angle?

c) What you observed in b) is called “total internal reflection.” What is reflected totally, and where?

9. It is possible to bend a long, rectangular BLOX so the light enters the narrow end of the BLOX, reflects off one side of the BLOX, then reflects off the other and back again to finally emerge from the other narrow end. Try to bend a BLOX rectangle so that the light is reflected as described.

FOR YOU TO READ

Snell's Law

Light refracts (bends) when it goes from air into another substance. This is true whether the other substance is gelatin, glass, water or diamond. The amount of bending is dependent on the material that the light enters. Each material has a specific index of refraction, *n*. This index of refraction is a property of the material and is one way in which a diamond (very high index of refraction—lots of bending) can be distinguished from glass (lower index of refraction—less bending). The index of refraction is a ratio of the sine of the angle of incidence and the sine of the angle of refraction.

Index of refraction: $n = \dfrac{\sin \angle i}{\sin \angle R}$

This equation is referred to as Snell's Law.

As light enters a substance from air, the light bends towards the normal. When light leaves a substance and enters air, it bends away from the normal. If the light is entering air from a substance, the angle in that substance may be such that the angle of refraction is 90°. In this special case, the angle in the substance is called the critical angle. If the angle in the substance is greater than this critical angle, then the light does not enter the air but reflects back into the substance as if the surface were a perfect mirror. This is the basis for light fibers where laser light reflects off the inner walls of glass and travels down the fiber, regardless of the bend in the fiber.

REFLECTING ON THE ACTIVITY AND THE CHALLENGE

The bending of light as it goes from air into a substance or from a substance into air is called refraction. It is mathematically expressed by Snell's Law. When light enters the substance at an angle, it bends towards the normal. When light leaves the substance at an angle, it bends away from the normal. As you create your light show for the chapter challenge, you may find creative uses of refraction. You may decide to have light bending in such a way that it spells out a letter or word or creates a picture. You may wish to have the light travel from air into glass to change its direction. You may have it bend by different amounts by replacing one material with another. Regardless of how you use refraction effects, you can now explain the physics principles behind them.

PHYSICS TO GO

1. A light ray goes from air into BLOX. In general, which is larger, the angle of incidence or the angle of refraction?

2. a) Make a sketch of a ray of light as it enters a piece of BLOX and is refracted.

   b) Now turn the ray around so it goes backwards. What was the angle of refraction is now the angle of incidence. Does the turned-around ray follow the path of the original ray?

3. A light ray enters BLOX from air. Make a diagram to show the angle of incidence, the angle of refraction, and the normal at the edge of the BLOX.

4. Light rays enter the BLOX from air. Make drawings to show rays with angles of incidence of 30° and 60°. For each incident ray, sketch the refracted ray that passes through the BLOX.

5. a) Light is passing from air into a BLOX. What is the maximum possible angle of incidence that will permit light to pass into the BLOX?

   b) Make a sketch to show your answer for part (a). Include the refracted ray (inside the BLOX) in your sketch.

6. a) A ray of light is already inside a BLOX and is heading out. What is the name of the maximum possible angle of incidence that will permit the light to pass out of the BLOX?

   b) If you make the angle of incidence in part (a) greater than this special angle, what happens to the light?

   c) Make a sketch to show your answer for part (b). Be sure to show what happened to the light.

7. a) Make a drawing of a light ray that enters the front side of a rectangular piece of BLOX and leaves through the back side.

   b) What is the relationship between the direction of the ray that enters the BLOX and the direction of the ray that leaves the BLOX?

   c) Use geometry, and your answer to question 2 (b), to prove your answer to part 7 (b).

8. You have seen the colored bands that a prism or cut glass or water produce from sunlight. Light that you see as different colors has different wavelengths. Since refraction makes these bands, what can you say about the way light of different wavelengths refracts?

STRETCHING EXERCISES

1. Prepare a BLOX with red-colored water. Shine a red laser beam into the BLOX, as you did in For You To Do, steps 1 through 3. What happens? How can you explain what happens?

2. Find some $\frac{1}{2}$" diameter clear tubing, about 2 m long. Plug one end. Pour clear gelatin in the other end, through a funnel, before the gelatin has had time to set. Arrange the tubing into an interesting shape and let the gelatin set. You may wish to mount your tube on a support or a sturdy piece of cardboard, which can be covered with interesting reflective material. Fasten one end of the tube so laser light can easily shine straight into it. When the gelatin has set, turn on the laser. What do you see? This phenomena is called total internal reflection.

3. Place a penny in the bottom of a dish or glass. Position your eye so you can just see the penny over the rim of the glass. Predict what will happen when you fill the glass with water. Then try it and see what happens. How can you explain the results?

Add water

4. Place an empty, clear drinking glass over a piece of a newspaper. When you look through the side of the glass near the bottom, you can see the printing on the newspaper. What do you think will happen if you fill the glass with water? Try it and see. How can you explain the result? Does it help to hold your fingers over the back of the glass?

Activity Eight

Effect of Lenses on Light

WHAT DO YOU THINK?

Engineers have created special lenses that can photograph movie scenes lit only by candlelight.

- **How is a lens able to project movies, take photographs, or help people with vision problems?**

Record your ideas about this question in your *Active Physics log*. Be prepared to discuss your responses with your small group and with your class.

FOR YOU TO DO

1. Look at the lens your teacher has given you.

   a) Make a side-view drawing of this lens in your log. This is a *convex* lens.

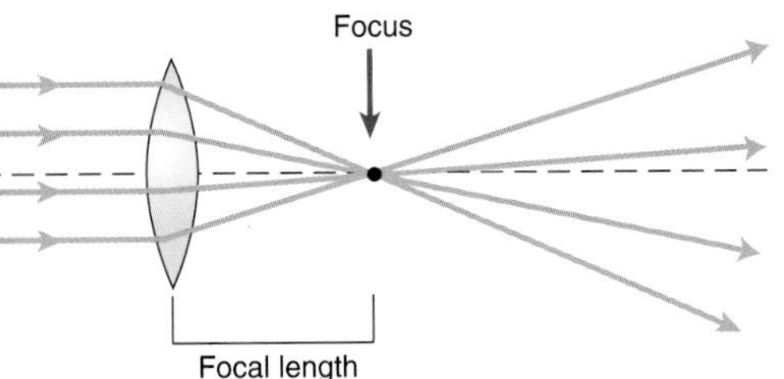

2. Point the lens at a window or at something distant outside. Use a file card as a screen. Look for the image on the file card. Move it back and forth until you see a sharp image of the distant object.
   a) Describe what you see. Is the image large or small? Is it right-side-up or upside-down? Is it reversed left-to-right? This image is called "real" because you can project it on the screen.

3. Measure the distance between the image and the lens. If the object is very far away, this distance is the focal length of the lens. The position of this image is the focus of the lens. It is the same location that parallel rays of light would converge.
   a) Approximate the object distance.
   b) Measure the image distance.
   c) Record your object and image distance. Note that the image distance is also the focal length of the lens.

Do not use lenses with chipped edges. Mount lenses securely in a holder. Use only light sources with enclosed or covered electrical contacts. Keep flammables/combustibles away from the candle holder.

4. Set up a 40-W light bulb or a candle to be a light source. Mount the lens at the same height as the light source. If you are using a light bulb, point it right at the lens, as shown.

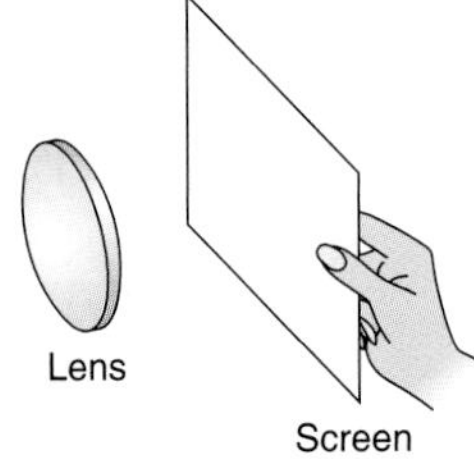

5. Place the light bulb about a meter away from the lens. Try to find the image of the light bulb on a screen. The screen can be a file card or a sheet of paper.
   a) Record your results in a table including the distance and appearance of the image.

6. Adjust the position of the object to create a larger image.
   a) Describe how the position of the object, the image, and the size of the image have changed. Record the results. in a table.

7. Create an object by carefully cutting a hole in the shape of an arrow in an index card. Have someone in your group hold the card close to the light bulb.

   a) Can you see the object on the screen? Describe what you see.

   b) Have the person holding the object move it around between the light bulb and the convex lens. What happens?

8. Project the object onto the wall. Can you make what you project larger or smaller?

   a) In your log indicate what you did to change the size of the image.

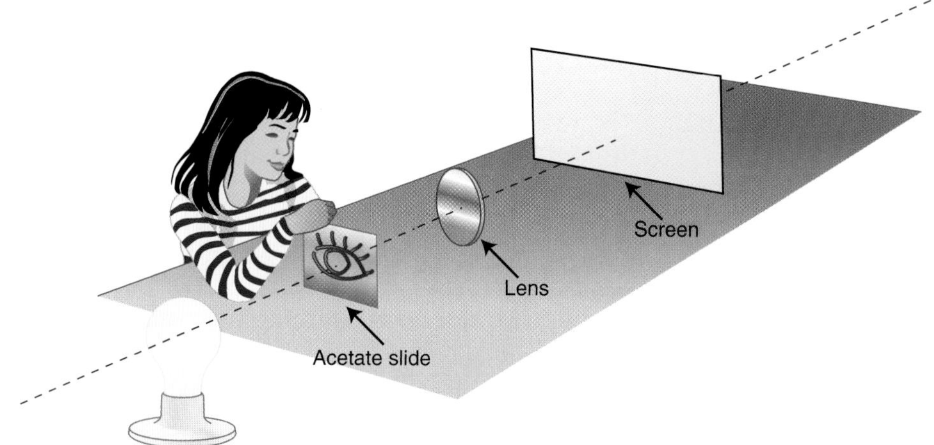

9. Create a slide by drawing with a marking pen on clear acetate. Try placing a 100-watt light bulb and the slide in different positions.

   a) Describe how you can project a real, enlarged image of your slide onto a screen or wall.

   b) How can you use the lens to change the size of the image?

   c) Explore the effect of different lenses. In your log record how you think this effect might be part of your light and sound show.

Caution: Lamps get very hot. Be careful not to touch the bulb or housing surrounding the bulb.

REFLECTING ON THE ACTIVITY AND THE CHALLENGE

You have explored how convex lenses make real images. You have found these images on a screen by moving a card back and forth until the image was sharp and clear, so you know that they occur at a particular place. Bringing the object near the lens moves the image away from the lens and enlarges the image, but if the object is too close to the lens, there is no real image. Also, these images are reversed left-to-right and are upside-down. You may be able to use this kind of image in your sound and light show. Also, you have projected images of slides on a wall. You may be able to add interest by moving the lens and screen to change the size of these images.

PHYSICS TO GO

1. a) What is the focus of a lens?
   b) If the image of an object is at the focus on a lens, where is the object located?
   c) What is the focal length of a lens?
   d) How can you measure the focal length of a lens?

2. a) You set up a lens and screen to make an image of a distant light. Is the image in color?
   b) Is the image right-side-up or upside-down?
   c) Did the lens bend light to make this image? How can you tell?
   d) A distant light source begins moving towards a lens. What must you do to keep the image sharp?

3. a) You make an image of a light bulb. What can you do to make the image smaller than the light bulb?
   b) What can you do to make the image larger than the light bulb?

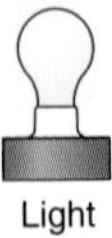

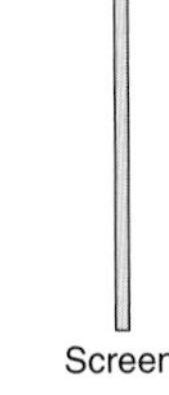

4. a) You have two lights, a lens, and a screen, as shown. One light is at a great distance from the lens. The other light is much closer. If you see a sharp image of the distant light, describe the image of the closer light.
   b) If you see a sharp image of the closer light, describe the image of the more distant light.
   c) Could you see a sharp image of both lights at the same time? Explain how you found your answer.

5. Research how a camera works. Find out where the image is located. Also find out how the lens changes so that you can photograph a distant landscape and also photograph people close-up.

STRETCHING EXERCISES

1. To investigate how the image position depends on the object position, find a convex lens, a white card, and a light source. Find the image of the light source, and measure the image and object distance from the lens. Make these measurements for as wide a range of object distances as you can. In addition, make an image of an object outside, like a tree. Estimate the distance to the tree. The image of a distant object, like the tree, is located very near the focus of the lens. Draw a graph of the results. Compare the graph with the equation

$$\frac{1}{f} = \frac{1}{D_o} + \frac{1}{D_i}$$

2. Find a camera with a shutter that you can keep open (with a bulb or time setting). Place a piece of wax paper or a piece of a plastic bag behind the lens, where the film would be if you took a picture. Find the image and compare it to the images you made in this activity. Focus the lens for objects at different distances. Investigate how well the object and image location fit the lens equation $\frac{1}{f} = \frac{1}{D_o} + \frac{1}{D_i}$.

   Remember that the focal length of the lens is typically printed on the lens.

3. Research how the concept of "depth of field" is important in photography. Report to the class on what you learn.

Activity Nine

Color

WHAT DO YOU THINK?

When a painter mixes red and green paint, the result is a dull brown. But when a lighting designer in a theater shines a red and a green light on an actress, the actress' skin looks bright yellow.

- **How could these two results be so different?**
- **How are the colors you see produced?**

Record your ideas about these questions in your *Active Physics log*. Be prepared to discuss your responses with your small group and with your class.

FOR YOU TO DO

1. Carefully cut out a cardboard puppet that you will use to make shadows.

2. Turn on a white light bulb only. Move the puppet around and observe the shadow.

a) Describe the shadow you see.

b) What happens to the shadow if you move the puppet sideways or up-and-down?

c) What happens to the shadow if you move the puppet close to the screen?

d) What happens to the shadow if you move the puppet close to the bulb?

Caution: Lamps get very hot. Be careful not to touch the bulb or housing surrounding the bulb.

3. Look at the drawing. It shows a top view of a puppet halfway between the light and the screen.

a) Make a copy of this drawing in your log. Draw light rays going from the light to the screen. (Light rays will go in straight lines in all directions from all parts of the light.)

b) Use the top-view drawing you drew to answer these questions: Which part of the screen receives light? Which part receives no light? Which part receives some light?

c) Is the shadow larger or smaller than the puppet? Explain how you found your answer.

d) Now copy the other two top-view drawings and show the path of the light rays.

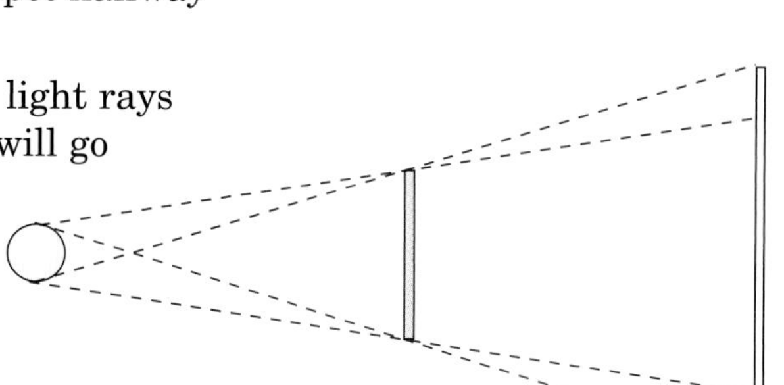

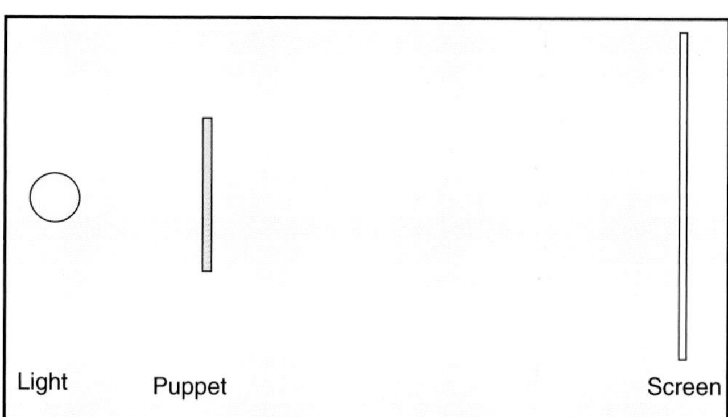

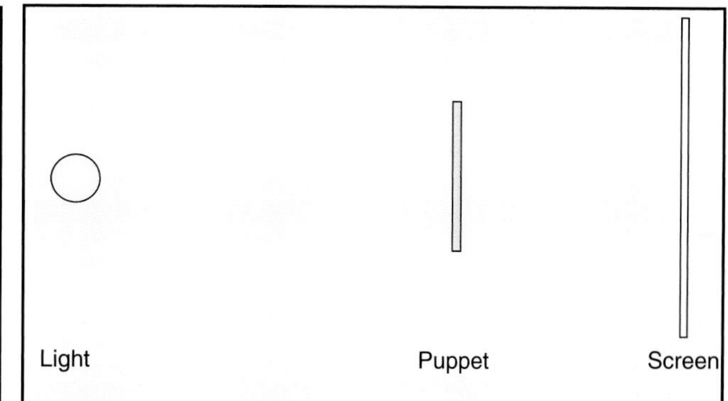

e) On your drawings, show which part of the screen does receive light and which part does not receive light and which part receives some light.

f) For each of these two drawings, tell if the shadow is larger or smaller than the puppet. For each one, explain how you found your answer.

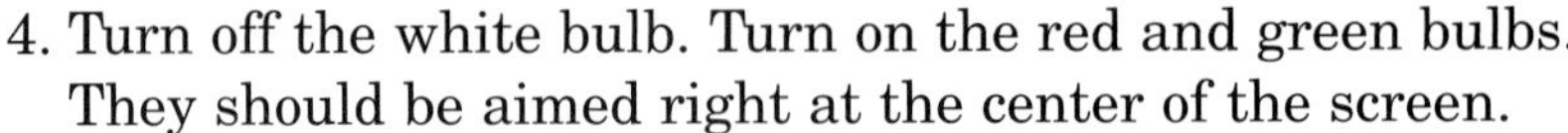

4. Turn off the white bulb. Turn on the red and green bulbs. They should be aimed right at the center of the screen.
   a) What color do you see on the screen?
   b) Predict what color the shadows will be if you bring your puppet between the bulbs and the screen. Record your prediction, and give a reason for it.
   c) Make a top-view drawing to show the path of the light rays from the red and green bulbs.
   d) On your drawing, label the color you will see on each part of the screen.

5. Turn off the green bulb and turn on the blue one. Repeat what you did in the previous step 4, but with the blue and red bulbs lit.

6. Turn off the red bulb and turn on the green one. Repeat what you did in step 4, but with the blue and green bulbs lit.

7. Turn on the red bulb so all three—red, blue, and green—are lit. Repeat what you did in steps 5 and 6.

REFLECTING ON THE ACTIVITY AND THE CHALLENGE

Different colored lights can combine to make white light. When an object blocks all light it creates a dark shadow. Since some light comes from all parts of the bulb, there are places where the shadow is black (no light) and places where the shadow is gray (some light reaches this area.) An object illuminated by different colored lights can create shadows which prevent certain colors from reaching the wall and allowing other colors to pass by.

In your light show creation, you may choose to use the ideas of colored shadows to show how lights can add to produce interesting combinations of colors. By moving the object or the lights during the show, you may be able to produce some interesting effects. Lighting design is used in all theater productions. It requires a knowledge and understanding of how lights work, as well as an aesthetic sense of what creates an enjoyable display.

PHYSICS TO GO

1. Show how a shadow is created.

2. How can moving the light, the object, and the screen all produce the effect of enlarging the shadow?

3. Explain why a gray halo surrounds a dark shadow made by a light bulb and an object.

4. a) Why is your shadow different at different times of the day?
   b) What is the position of the sun when your shadow is the longest? The shortest?

5. Why is the gray halo about your shadow so thin when you are illuminated by the sun?

6. a) Suppose you shine a red light on a screen in a dark room. The result is a disk of red light. Now you turn on a green light and a blue light. The three disks of light overlap as shown. Copy the diagram into your journal. Label the color you will see in each part of the diagram.

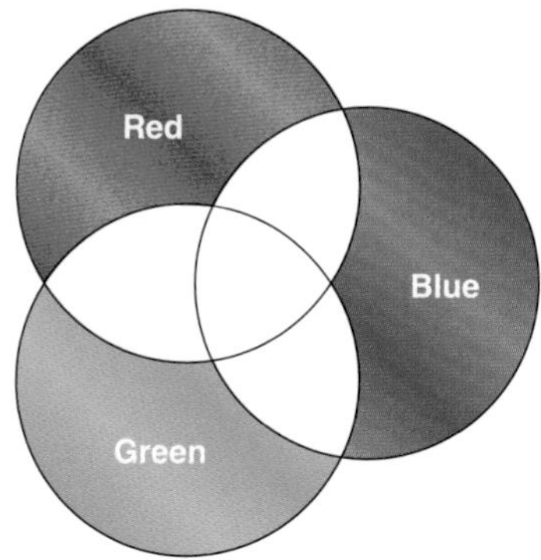

   b) Add the labels "bright", "brighter", and "brightest" to describe what you would see in each part of your diagram.

7. a) Make a drawing of an object in red light. The object casts a shadow on the screen. Label the color of the shadow and the rest of the screen.
   b) Repeat part (a) for an object in green light.
   c) Now make a copy of your drawing for part (b). Add a red light, as in part (a). Label the color of all the shadows.

8. List some imaginative ways that you can add colors to your light show.

STRETCHING EXERCISES

1. With the room completely dark, shine a red light on various colored objects. Compare the way they look in red light with the way they look in ordinary room light.

2. View 3-D pictures with red and blue glasses. Explain how each eye sees a different picture.

3. Shine a white light and a red light on a small object in front of a screen. What colors are the shadows? How is this surprising?

4. Prepare a large drawing of the American flag but with blue-green in the place of red, and yellow in the place of blue. Stare at the drawing for 30 s and then look at a white surface.

PHYSICS AT WORK

Alicja and Dennis Phipps

Alicja Phipps has always been interested in electronics. As a child she wanted to be a television repair person. She now works along with her husband, Dennis Phipps, in their company Light & Sound Entertainment which designs original content programming in a variety of areas—from rock concerts to the Olympics.

Light & Sound Entertainment got its name because Dennis believes strongly that the two are, and should be linked. "It's terrible when the music of a production does not match what you are seeing," he says. "More and more theaters have lighting specialists come in and set up the theater with everything preset on a computerized lighting board. There will be a setting for 'outdoor lighting' and 'nighttime' or 'sunset'. The problem with that is that every production will look the same when in reality nighttime in Canada looks very different from nighttime in Florida. There are also different lighting considerations depending on your audience. A production in front of a live audience needs different lighting than one being recorded on video. For instance, the human eye picks up shadows a lot better than a camera will. If a production is intended for both a live audience and video, lighting needs to be arranged accordingly."

"The sound of a production is only as good as its setup," he continues, "and nothing can replace the actual setting. The Red Rock Theater in California is terrific, for example, because stone has a very high reverberation rate which is great for guitars. A huge wooden room like Carnegie Hall also provides a unique sound. However these spaces and materials are not readily available." The hardest projects, Dennis says, are those in which you cannot control the elements. "Sound elements include the size and shape of the space, reverberation, feedback, and temperature."

"New media," explains Alicja who oversees the conversion of live events into various other formats such as CD-ROMs, virtual reality, and web sites, "has its own set of challenges. We have to think about how much information (sound and image) we will be able to fit on a disc or on to a web page and how long it will take to load. If it takes too long no one will ever see or hear what we've done."

"We enjoy the creative process of every production," claim Alicja and Dennis, "each one is a unique challenge."

Chapter 1 Assessment

With what you learned about sound and light in this chapter you are now ready to dazzle the world. However, you have neither the funds nor the technology available to professionals. All sounds you use to capture the interest of the class must come from musical instruments that you build yourself, or from human voices. Some of these sounds may be prerecorded and then played in your show. If your teacher has a laser and is willing to allow you to use it, you may do so. All other light must come from conventional household lamps. Gather with your committee to design a two- to four-minute sound and light show to entertain other students your age.

Review the criteria by which you decided that your show will be evaluated. The following suggestions were provided at the beginning of the chapter:

1. The variety and number of physics concepts used to produce the light and sound effects.
2. Your understanding of the physics concepts:
   a) Name the physics concepts that you used.
   b) Explain each concept.
   c) Give an example of something that each concept explains or an example of how each concept is used.
   d) Explain why each concept is important.
3. Entertainment value.

At this time you may wish to propose changes in the criteria. Also, decide as a class if you wish to modify or keep the point value you established at the beginning of the chapter.

Enjoy the sound and light productions!

Physics You Learned

Compressional and transverse waves

Wave speed = wavelength × frequency

Standing waves

Pitch and frequency

Sound production in pipes and vibrating strings

Controlling frequency of sounds produced electronically

Angle of incidence and angle of reflection

Location of image in plane and curved mirrors

$\frac{1}{f} = \frac{1}{D_o} + \frac{1}{D_i}$ in curved mirrors

Real images

Angle of incidence and angle of refraction

Lenses and image formation

$\frac{1}{f} = \frac{1}{D_o} + \frac{1}{D_i}$ in lenses

Color addition

$n = \frac{\sin\angle i}{\sin\angle R}$

LONG-DISTANCE COMMUNICATION

Scenario

You are always communicating with others. You talk to your friends at school. You call them on the telephone. You may show photographs of special events or people to them. You may send letters or e-mail, to those who have moved away. Or, you may have made new friends, many miles distant, by communicating through the Internet.

No matter how you communicate, you require a code. Language and pictures are codes you learn from an early age. Talking may feel as natural to you as breathing. But many years ago you had to learn to translate your thoughts and feelings into a code that those close to you could understand. In order to communicate with others you are continually translating your thoughts from one code to another. Code and communication are forever linked.

Challenge

1. You are a member of a team of engineers who is developing a communications system. The system must communicate from one room to the next. Since this system is a model for long-distance communication, assume that the other room is far away. Yelling and waving will not work. The requirement is that you are able to send and receive a message. You will have to divide your team into senders and receivers, with the receivers in the other room. You will have about five minutes to set up your system before you test it to meet the requirement. During the test, you must measure the speed of transmission of your system.

   In this test, the message you will communicate will be simple and brief and may include either text, picture, music, or a combination of these.

After a successful test, each team member will submit a written report about the system. This report will have the following parts:

a) the design of the system
b) how your method of communication is better for this challenge than the other methods you investigated in this chapter
c) the physics of your system
d) your measurement of the speed of transmission in words per minute, symbols per minute, or notes per minute.

2. Every day you hear about the Internet. It seems every business and many people have Web pages and e-mail accounts. You can buy books, CDs, or plane tickets on the Internet. You can even bank and buy and sell stocks on the Internet. The Internet is a busy place with a lot of money changing hands. Write an essay that deals with either of the following concerns.

    a) As more people use the Internet for shopping, banking, and business, criminals may use the Internet too. What kind of crime might happen on the Internet? What can be done to prevent people from "listening in" or from stealing information? Who should prevent it?
    b) Society has decided that some books and movies are not right for children. There are no such restrictions on the Internet. Should children use the Internet as they wish, without any limits? Or should they be restricted in some way? How could these limits be set up? Who should decide?

Criteria

As a class, discuss how you wish your work to be evaluated. You can use the following criteria, with suggested point values, as a starting point in your discussion.

Your communication system will be graded in two ways:

A grade will be assigned to the speed and quality of the transmission. You can determine the speed and quality by recording how much of the message was correctly transmitted. 40 points

The quality of your written report will also be graded. 60 points

a) explanation of design (including drawings) 15 points
b) how your method is better than others you thought of 15 points
c) the physics of your system 25 points
d) your measurement of the speed of transmission of your system 5 points

Your essay will be graded mainly on how well you present the social issues. If you add helpful technical information about the Internet, that can earn additional credit. With your class members, decide on a marking scheme for your essay.

Activity One

Using Waves to Communicate

WHAT DO YOU THINK?

A substantial prize was offered fifty years ago for the first person who could develop a new language. Nobody has yet been able to claim that prize.

- **How are animals able to communicate?**
- **Would their communication satisfy your definition of language?**

Record your ideas about these questions in your *Active Physics log*. Be prepared to discuss your responses with your small group and with your class.

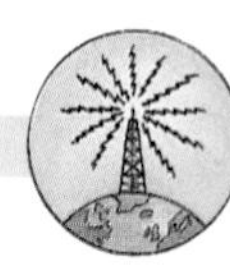

FOR YOU TO DO

1. Fill a large pan with water to about 5 cm of the top. Add a few drops of food coloring and mix. Float a tiny piece of paper in the pan. When the water is calm, touch the center of the water surface with the tip of a pen or pencil. Observe the pulse and the piece of paper.
   a) What is the shape of the pulse?
   b) What happens to the piece of paper as the pulse passes by?

2. With a partner, stretch out a slinky on a cleared area of the floor. Have your partner hold the other end of the slinky firmly, so it cannot move. Make a pulse by snapping your end of the spring back and forth along the floor, like cracking a whip.
   a) What happens to the pulse when it reaches the other end of the spring?
   b) How is the reflected pulse similar to the original pulse? How is it different?
   c) Which way does the pulse move?
   d) Imagine you put a small piece of tape on one part of the spring. How does the tape move as the pulse goes by?
   e) Once the wave has passed, what has happened to the slinky? How has it changed from before the pulse went by?

3. With your partner, figure out a way to send a message on the slinky. The message can be as simple as "yes" or "no," or "0" or "1." It can be as complex as an idea or an emotion. You may need to make a code to deliver your message.
   a) State the message you are going to send.
   b) Give the message in the code you use.
   c) Describe how the message is transmitted.
   d) Tell how the receiver converts the code to the message.
   e) What is difficult about sending the message?
   f) Measure the time required to send the message.

4. To try another way to send a message, make cup phones. Take two plastic cups and a 4-m long string. Carefully punch a small hole in the bottom of each cup and push one end of the string through the hole. Tie a knot in each end of the string.

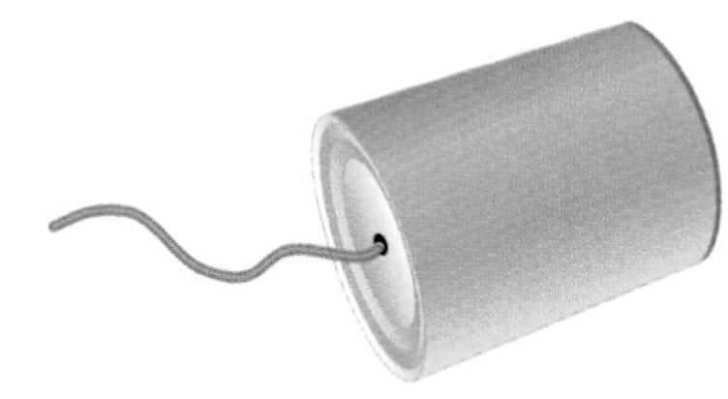

5. Walk away from your partner until the string is tight. Hold your hands around the cup so your partner can't hear you directly.
   a) When you talk, what does your partner hear through the cup phone?

6. Now create a message and try to send it with the cup phone. Take turns talking and listening.
   a) Are you able to hear the message?
   b) How well is the message transmitted?
   c) How does changing the string tension change the quality of the transmission?
   d) Do soft sounds transmit as well as loud sounds?
   e) If you coded your message, describe the code.
   f) Try to modify the cup phone to improve the quality of the transmission.
   g) Measure the time required to send your message.

7. Make a code for your cup phone so you can send a message without using your voice. Compare communication using the code with communication using voice.
   a) How does communicating using a code differ?
   b) How far could a cup phone transmit a message? Make a prediction. Record what you think will happen.

8. Test your prediction from step 7.
   a) Record the result.

9. Use a third cup and string to eavesdrop on a message that is being transmitted on the cup phone.
   a) How well does the third cup work?
   b) Can the receiver and sender detect if their call is being monitored?

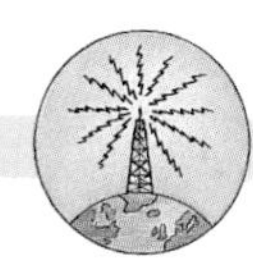

REFLECTING ON THE ACTIVITY AND THE CHALLENGE

In this activity you were able to invent a code and transmit messages using that code. In transmitting the code along the slinky, you observed that the slinky remained in the same place after the message was transmitted. In the cup phone, you used an existing code, language, and transmitted the message. Once again, the cup phone remained in the same place while the message traveled from one cup to another. You also investigated the properties of slinkies and cup phones in order to find out how to optimize their performance. Finally you tried to eavesdrop using a third cup.

In the chapter challenge you will be required to send a message from one room to another. The slinky or cup phone may work with modification. As you learn other techniques for transmitting messages, you will begin to understand when slinkies and cup phones are the best technology. The challenge also requires you to write an essay about secrecy on the Internet. Your experience with eavesdropping in a cup phone may provide some help with this essay.

PHYSICS TO GO

1. a) You are wading in a river and watching water waves washing over your feet. If one wave washes over your feet every two seconds, what is the frequency of the waves?
   b) You watch the waves out on the river before they hit your feet. The distance from one wave crest to the next crest is 5 m. What is the wavelength of the wave?
   c) Predict the speed of this wave.

2. a) In the For You To Do, you made a pulse on the slinky. What happened to the pulse when it reflected from one end of the slinky?
   b) Predict how a water wave would reflect if the wave hit a sea wall.
   c) Run a little water in a bathtub. Push the water to make a "pulse," and watch what happens when the pulse hits the end of the tub. How does your prediction compare to what happened?
   d) Does the water pulse reflect in the same way as the slinky pulse?

Lean over the side of the tub and push the water with your hands. Do not stand in the tub.

3. When the slinky pulse moved past a point on the slinky, the spring moved from its normal position and then returned. Compare this movement of the spring with the movement of water when a wave passes by.

4. Compare the cup phone to a telephone. How are they similar? How are they different?

5. Predict what would happen if you changed the size of the cup on the cup phone. How could you test your prediction?

6. You may have heard of a washtub bass. In this instrument, a metal washtub sits upside down on the ground. A single metal string is fastened to the top of a metal washtub. The performer plucks this string. How is a washtub bass similar to a cup phone? How is it different?

7. Compare your code for the slinky with your speech for the cup phone. Describe two advantages for each code.

8. What limits the speed of sending code through the slinky? How can you improve the speed?

9. When the "eavesdropping" cup was added to the cup phone, was this apparent to the other people? Is there a way to prevent this type of eavesdropping with cup phones?

10. a) Do you think that people eavesdrop on your telephone calls? Why or why not?
    b) What should be the penalty for eavesdropping?

11. Military secrets are sent from one place to another. How do you think that the military code their signal so that nobody will be able to eavesdrop on the message?

STRETCHING EXERCISES

What would happen if you used the cup phone outside and an owl perched on the string? Make a model of a perched owl. Predict the effect this model will have on cup phone communication. Then test your prediction.

Activity Two

Signals and Noise

WHAT DO YOU THINK?

It has been suggested that 95% of human communication happens without words.

- **When you talk with adults, why don't they always understand you?**
- **Do your friends always understand what you say? Why or why not?**
- **What happens when you try to exchange ideas with someone who doesn't speak your language?**

Record your ideas about these questions in your *Active Physics log*. Be prepared to discuss your responses with your small group and with your class.

FOR YOU TO DO

1. Imagine the great Pharaoh of Egypt in his palace. He has just approved a model of a stone monument that his architect has designed. They both want to begin work as soon as possible. His building supervisor is already in the desert, ready to begin work. Bringing the building supervisor back to the palace would waste too much time. How can the Pharaoh and his architect communicate the plan to the building supervisor? Assume some sort of "telephone" hook-up between the architect and the building supervisor. With a partner, assume the roles of Pharaoh's architect and building supervisor.

2. Divide a set of building bricks so you each have an identical set of bricks. Set up a curtain of books or cardboard between you and your partner.

3. The architect constructs a model of the monument, but without allowing the building supervisor to see the model. The model should be an original design. Do not simply build a pyramid. The architect then gives verbal directions to the builder over the curtain between them. The supervisor builds a model based on these directions. The supervisor can ask questions, but neither the architect nor the supervisor can see each other's model.

4. When you have completed the exercise, compare the builder's model to the architect's model. Add up the total number of correctly placed blocks. Also add up the total number of blocks in the architect's model. To get one number that describes the success of the communication, find the fraction of correctly placed blocks:

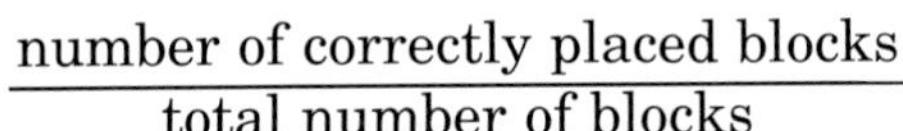

$$\frac{\text{number of correctly placed blocks}}{\text{total number of blocks}}$$

a) Write the fraction as a decimal number.

5. Play a game like "Wheel of Fortune." Your teacher will make up a phrase or expression and put spaces for each letter on the board. Take turns choosing letters that might be in the phrase.

6. Before you begin the next game, record the total number of spaces for the letters in a table like the one shown. Notice the column in the table labeled "Number of letters showing." At the beginning of the game, this number is zero. At the end of the game, all the letters are showing.

Number of letters showing	Prediction of number of students who can guess the phrase	Number of students who can guess the phrase

a) Fill in the "Number of letters showing" column up to the total number of letters in the phrase. Predict how many students will guess the phrase when each number of letters is showing. Of course, when the number is zero, no letters are showing, and probably no one in the class will be able to guess the phrase. When all the letters are showing, everyone in the class can read the phrase.

7. As you play this time, continue to choose letters out loud. But do not guess the phrase out loud.

a) In your log, write down the blanks for the letters. Each time you make a guess, record the guess and the number of letters. Circle the number of letters that were showing when you guessed correctly.

8. Make a class graph on the board. Your teacher will ask, "Who got the answer after the first letter? After the second letter? . . ." The graph will show the number of letters as the independent variable (on the horizontal axis). The dependent variable (on the vertical axis) is the total number of students who have correctly guessed the phrase.

a) Make a copy of the graph for your log.

REFLECTING ON THE ACTIVITY AND THE CHALLENGE

Communicating an image with words can be quite difficult as you have observed in the architect-builder exercise. With practice, you would probably improve your ability to describe shapes with words. A picture, though, would always be more efficient. Some people can express themselves with images and create paintings to communicate their ideas. If they could express those ideas in words, perhaps we might not need art. But as you've seen, substituting words for images leads to lots of problems.

You also tried to communicate a word message without all of the letters. Some people are better at this than others. The success of this depends on a shared knowledge between the sender and receiver of the knowledge. A person could probably communicate the name Elvis Presley with only the first five letters if both people know the singer. If one has never heard of the singer, the entire name would have to be spelled out.

When you try to communicate your message in the chapter challenge, you may have to decide whether a picture or words are easier to send. You may also have to decide if there is a common experience that would allow you to send the message more efficiently. Common experiences may also be a way of ensuring that you have privacy. If you both know certain things that others do not know, you can use this to hide information and maintain secrecy. This could help you with your essay about privacy on the Internet.

PHYSICS TO GO

1. a) Identify the mistakes in communication between the architect and the building supervisor that your group made.
   b) Explain how each mistake happened.
   c) Suggest an improvement to the communication system you used. Explain how this change would prevent the mistake.

2. a) Give an example of a mistake in communication between you and another person.
   b) Explain how the mistake happened.
   c) Suggest an improvement to the communication system you and the other person used. Explain how the change would prevent the mistake.

3. Suppose the architect had given the building supervisor a drawing, but the two could not speak to each other. How well would they have communicated? Explain your answer.

4. a) Repeat the first part of Activity Two at home. Instead of a design of blocks, limit the design to stacks of pennies, nickels, and dimes.
   b) Is this activity easier or more difficult than the Pharaoh activity? Tell why.
   c) Could you communicate even better if you and your partner had agreed on a code in advance?

5. a) Suppose the Pharaoh's architect and building supervisor had agreed on a code in advance. How would that have changed the communication?
   b) If the building supervisor was blind, how would that have changed the communication? How could you change the activity to improve the communication?
   c) If the building supervisor was deaf, how would that have changed the communication? How could you change the activity to improve the communication?

Activity Three

The Electricity and Magnetism Connection

WHAT DO YOU THINK?

Earth's north pole has not always been in the same place. In fact, over many millions of years, the poles have actually reversed many times. The magnetic north pole has been near the geographic south pole.

- **How does a compass show which way is north?**

Record your ideas about this question in your *Active Physics log*. Be prepared to discuss your responses with your small group and with your class.

FOR YOU TO DO

1. Place a compass on the table. Wait until the needle stops moving. Bring a small magnet near the compass.
   a) Record your observations.

2. Move the magnet around slowly.
   a) What happens to the compass?

3. Create a code so that someone looking at the compass can read the code. The person reading the code can manipulate the compass from under a piece of paper.
   a) How fast can you send the code?

4. Remove the magnet. Place a wire on top of the compass, as shown. Briefly touch the ends of the wire to the ends of the battery.
   a) What happens to the compass needle?

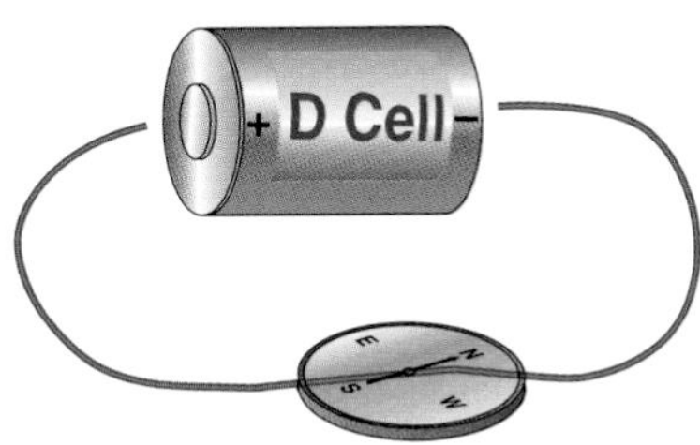

5. Create a setup where the wire is placed on the compass and the presence of a current creates a code. The code can then be read by observation of the compass.
   a) How fast can you send this code?
   b) Does this code have any advantages over the code in step 3?

6. Turn the wire to a different direction and repeat step 4.
   a) What happens this time? Try several different directions.

7. Obtain a 5-m length of wire and a cardboard tube. *Carefully* strip 1 cm of insulation from each end of the wire. Wrap the wire around the cardboard tube, with all turns going in the same direction. Before you start, leave about 30 cm on each end for making connections. Tape the coil of wire in place.

8. Connect the ends of the wire to a meter that measures small currents. This type of meter is called a *galvanometer*.

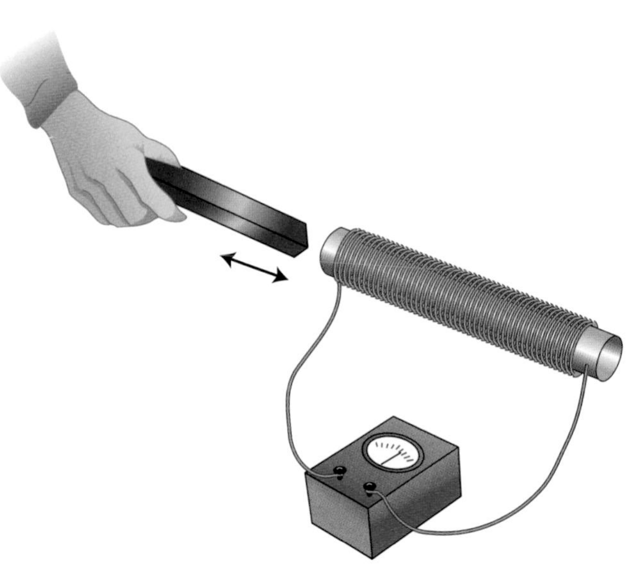

9. Push a bar magnet into the cardboard tube, as shown.
   - a) What happens?
   - b) Pull the magnet out of the tube. What happens?
   - c) Move the magnet in and out rapidly. What happens?
   - d) Hold the magnet still and move the coil back and forth. What happens?
   - e) Was a current produced when the magnet moved through the tube?
   - f) Was a current produced when the magnet was at rest inside the tube?
   - g) How was the direction that the magnet moved important?
   - h) Did it matter if the coil moved or if the magnet moved? Explain your answer.

10. Create a code that can be read by someone observing the current meter in step 8.
    - a) How fast can you send this code?
    - b) Does this code have any advantage over the codes used in steps 3 and 5?

11. Make electromagnets by wrapping wire around nails. Be sure the last few centimeters of insulation is sanded off each end of each wire. You will investigate the effect of the number of turns of wire. Wind each piece of wire tightly around a separate nail. For each nail, wind a different number of turns. Leave enough unwrapped wire at each end to connect to a cell. Tape each coil of wire in place.

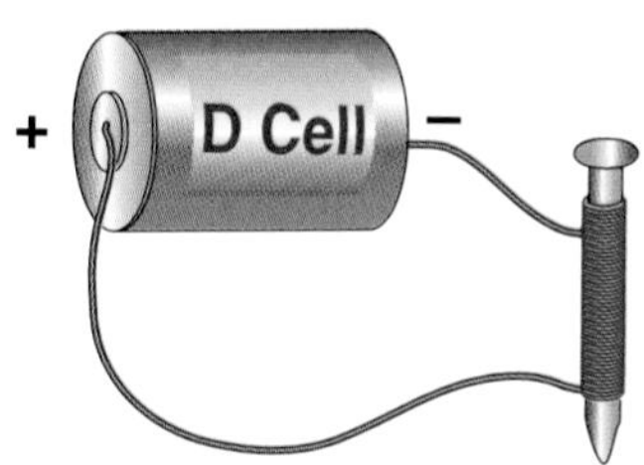

12. Hook up one coil to a battery as shown in the drawing. Figure out a way to measure the strength of your electromagnet. Hint: You can count how many paper clips or washers the electromagnet will pick up. Leave the battery connected for as short a time as possible to limit the battery's energy loss.

13. Connect several batteries together end-to-end, as in a flashlight. Make an electromagnet with these batteries.

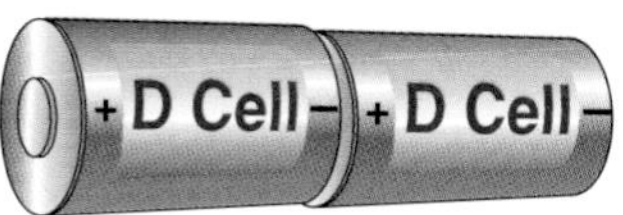

a) How does using several batteries change the strength of your electromagnet?

14. A digital code is a set of ones and zeroes. An analog code is a continuous set of numbers, like the number line in mathematics, between zero and one.

a) Which of the methods you investigated in this activity can be used for digital coding?

b) Which of the methods you investigated in this activity can be used for analog coding?

c) Which of the methods can be used for both?

d) What advantage would digital coding have over analog coding?

e) What advantage would analog coding have over digital coding?

REFLECTING ON THE ACTIVITY AND THE CHALLENGE

You have investigated a relationship between magnetism and electricity. A magnet affects a compass as does an electric current. You have also created electricity by moving a magnet past a coil of wire. Finally, you have made an electromagnet by using current to create the magnet. Each of these mechanisms was then used by you to code a message. Some of these approaches were limited to digital codes while others could be digital or analog codes.

In setting up your communication system for the chapter challenge, you may decide to use one of these techniques. You will have to decide whether your code should be digital or analog. You may also view one of these methods as a way to prevent a message from being transmitted. This may be important in maintaining secrecy in the second part of your challenge.

PHYSICS TO GO

1. a) If you place a compass on the table, which way does the compass needle point?
   b) What happened to the compass needle when an electric current ran through the wire?
   c) Does the current in the wire make the compass point in a particular direction? Can you identify that direction?
   d) In step 6, you turned the wire in many different directions. Was there one direction where the electric current did not change the compass? Provide an explanation for this.
   e) In step 12 you connected together several batteries end-to-end and investigated their effect on the electromagnet. Predict what would have happened if you had done that in the activity with the wire and the compass.

2. a) Make a drawing to show a compass under a wire.
   b) Draw the compass when the wires are connected to a battery.
   c) Draw the compass when the wires in part (b) are reversed.

3. a) In this activity, you made a coil to investigate how a moving magnet can produce electric current. What would have happened if you had just used a straight wire?
   b) In step 3, you ran a current through a straight wire to investigate the effect on a compass. Predict what would have happened if you had used a much longer wire and wound it into a coil.

4. Predict what would happen if you brought the compass near the electromagnet.

5. a) List the variables that affect the strength of an electromagnet.
   b) Briefly, tell how you would investigate each variable.

6. Review the steps in this activity where you used a coil of wire. What effect did the coil of wire have in each case?

7. a) Locate the circuit breaker box or fuse box in your home.
   b) With the help of an adult, find out how the switches, fuses, or breakers work.

8. a) Sketch your electric meter, including the readings on the dials and the positions of the hands. Date your sketch.
   b) One week later, sketch the meter and the readings again.
   c) Figure out how much electricity you used in that week.

STRETCHING EXERCISES

1. Investigate the effect of wrapping a coil around a compass and running current through the coil. Find out the effect of changing the number of turns in the coil. Also find out the effect of adding a second coil with the same number of turns as the first.

2. Build a compass by magnetizing a paper clip and floating it on water. Find out what happens when you bring a coil of wire near the compass and using a battery run current through the coil.

3. Investigate how an electromagnet affects a compass. Also, investigate how two electromagnets affect each other, and how two compasses affect each other. Write a summary of everything you have discovered.

Activity Four

Making the Connection

WHAT DO YOU THINK?

The first telegraph sent messages along a wire.

- **How do you think this telegraph worked?**
- **How do you think it was improved?**

Record your ideas about these questions in your *Active Physics log*. Be prepared to discuss your responses with your small group and with your class.

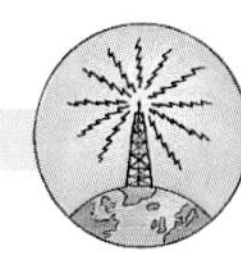

FOR YOU TO DO

Design Your Own Investigation

1. You are going to design and build a telegraph. Two people operate a telegraph—the sender and the receiver. The sender opens and closes a switch. The receiver, some distance away, observes whether a second switch opens or closes. Your telegraph must include both a sender and a receiver. Examine the list of materials that you can use.

   magnet wire (10 m)
   steel nails
   sandpaper
   wire cutter/stripper
   batteries (with a total of 6 V)
   plastic or flexible clips for connecting wires
   alligator clips for connecting wires
   key or normally open push button switch
   mounting board for transmitter and receiver
   small nuts and bolts

2. Work with your partner to make a plan.
   a) Make a drawing of your design.

3. With your teacher's approval, build your system and test it.
   a) How well did your system work?
   b) How could you improve your system? Remember that engineers and inventors are hardly ever satisfied with their first designs.

4. Improve your system and re-test it.
   a) Make a careful drawing of your system. Be sure to list all the materials you use.
   b) Explain how you improved your system over your first design.

5. Practice sending messages in Morse code. Part of the code is shown.

● is a dot; — is a dash

A	●—	**N**	—●	**1**	●————
B	—●●●	**O**	———	**2**	●●———
C	—●—●	**P**	●——●	**3**	●●●——
D	—●●	**Q**	——●—	**4**	●●●●—
E	●	**R**	●—●	**5**	●●●●●
F	●●—●	**S**	●●●	**6**	—●●●●
G	——●	**T**	—	**7**	——●●●
H	●●●●	**U**	●●—	**8**	———●●
I	●●	**V**	●●●—	**9**	————●
J	●———	**W**	●——	**0**	—————
K	—●—	**X**	—●●—	**.**	●—●—●—
L	●—●●	**Y**	—●——	**?**	●●——●●
M	——	**Z**	——●●		

6. Measure the time it takes to send a short message using the Morse code.
   a) Calculate the time needed to send one letter of the alphabet.
   b) How long do you think it would take to send 500 words by telegraph using the Morse code?

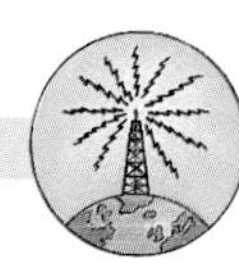

REFLECTING ON THE ACTIVITY AND THE CHALLENGE

You have designed and built a working telegraph. You may want to build a telegraph to meet the chapter challenge. Since you have made a careful drawing of your design, you can easily reassemble it. Or you may want to modify your design. Perhaps you will have additional materials when you meet the challenge, and you can change your design to use these materials.

PHYSICS TO GO

1. a) Explain in a few sentences how your telegraph works.
   b) Review the earlier activities in this chapter. How does what you learned in these activities help you explain the physics of the telegraph?

2. a) What would you like to improve about your telegraph design?
   b) If you had any materials you wanted, how could you improve your design?

3. a) Telegraph lines were first run along railroad tracks. Why was this a good place for the lines?
   b) Why was it good for the railroads to have the telegraph lines run along the railroad tracks?

4. a) Write a simple message.
   b) Write your message in Morse code.
   c) What are the advantages of Morse code?
   d) What are the disadvantages of Morse code?
   e) If you had to design a system to send messages with Morse code, how could you speed up the communication?

5. a) If you sent a message in Morse code, how would you show that a sentence had ended?
   b) How would you show that the whole message had ended?

6. a) You may know that computers work with binary numbers. In the binary number system, the only possible digits are zero and one. How is the binary number system similar to Morse code?
   b) The following are the binary numbers from 0 to 9:

0	0
1	1
2	10
3	11
4	100
5	101
6	110
7	111
8	1000
9	1001

   Write the binary numbers for 10 to 20.

7. Could the telegraph information be stolen? How could someone tap into the line and pick up your secret communication?

STRETCHING EXERCISE

Go to the library and look up how a telegraph key works. Also find out how a telegraph receiver works. Make a brief presentation to the class. Explain how this telegraph is an improvement over your telegraph.

Activity Five

Voice Signals

WHAT DO YOU THINK?

You can send your voice over a telephone line. You can also send computer information using a telephone and a modem. Using a fax machine and a telephone you can send images. You can even send video images using a telephone line.

- **How does a telephone work?**

Record your ideas about this question in your *Active Physics log*. Be prepared to discuss your responses with your small group and with your class.

FOR YOU TO DO

1. Check the ends of a 1-m long piece of magnet wire. Be sure that the last few centimeters have been sanded. Notice that the copper metal of the wire itself is a slightly different color than the orange insulation painted on the wire.

2. Make a coil with the magnet wire. The diameter should be about 2 cm. If a cardboard tube is available, wind the coil around the tube. Be sure to leave about 5 cm free at each end. Tape the coil together so it will not unwind.

3. Find the headphone plug with two wires coming out. Check to see that each end has an alligator clip.

4. Connect the alligator clips on the headphone plug to the ends of the coil. Be sure the coil wires are sanded at the point where the alligator clips make contact. If you have no alligator clips, *carefully* solder these wires together.

Caution: Soldering irons are very hot and can easily burn you.

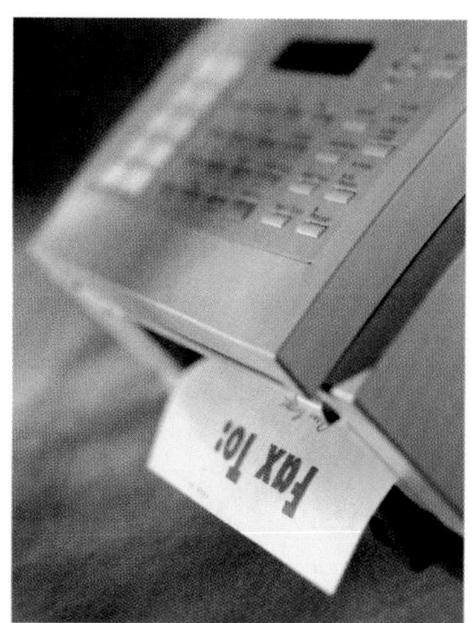

5. Tape the coil to the bottom of a cup, as shown.

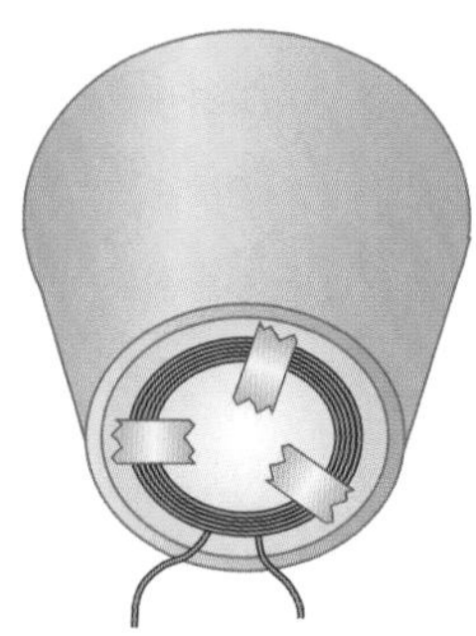

6. Turn on a personal stereo and tune the radio to a station. Push the plug into the earphone jack. Hold a magnet up to the coil. What do you hear?

a) Record your observations in your log.

b) Remove the magnet. What happens? Record the result.

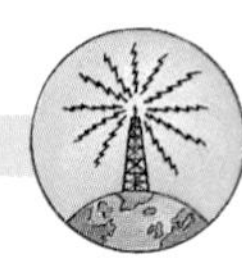

7. If you have an amplified speaker, insert the plug into the amplified speaker jack. After turning the amplifier on, speak into the cup. What do you hear?

   a) Record your results in your log. Try it with and without the magnet near the coil. If your words come out of the speaker, your cup has become a microphone.

8. Find the solar cell and earphone plug. Connect the solar cell leads to the earphone plug leads, with the alligator clips, as shown.

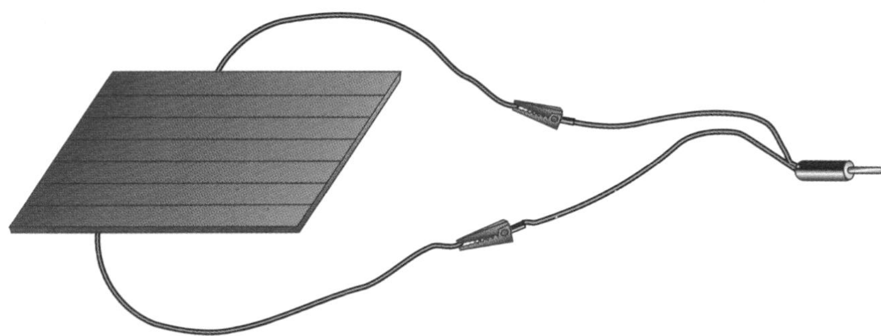

9. Insert the plug into the input of the amplifier/speaker, and turn the amplifier on. Point the solar cell toward the room lights. What do you hear?

   a) Record your observations. The solar cell is converting light into electricity.

10. Shine a flashlight beam at the solar cell. Move the beam off and on the cell. Try to send a short message in Morse code to your partner.

   a) What was the result?

   b) How far can you send a message this way?

FOR YOU TO READ

Speakers and Microphones

The radio sends a small amount of current through the earphone jack to the coil. This current changes thousands of times each second. The speaker moves when the charge flows, if the magnet is in place inside the speaker. The changing current makes the bottom of the cup vibrate, and this vibration produces sound. A microphone has the same design as a speaker. In the microphone, the vibration of your voice moves a coil of wire. Since there is a magnet next to the coil, this movement makes an electric current in the coil. That current becomes the signal that is sent through the wire.

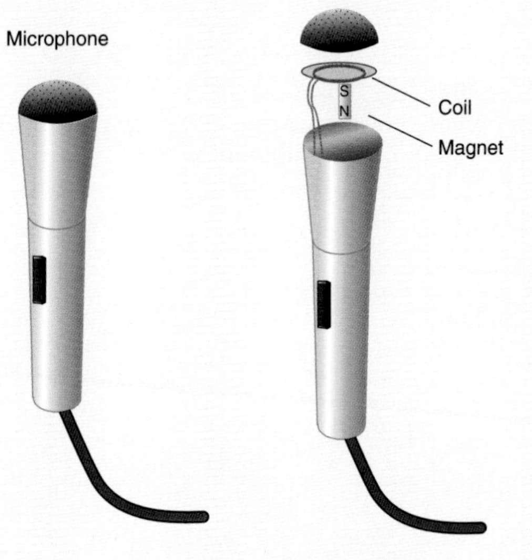

Speaker

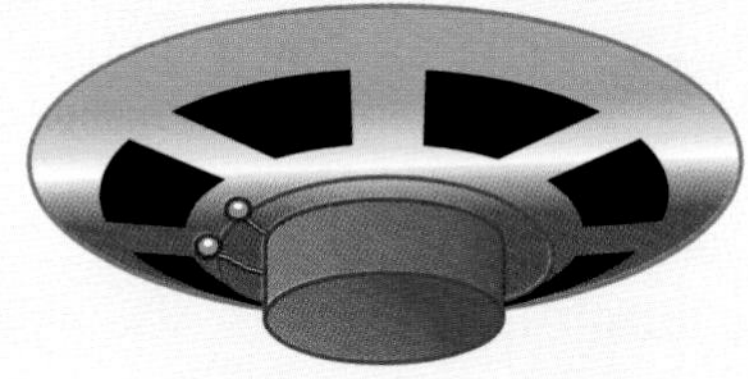

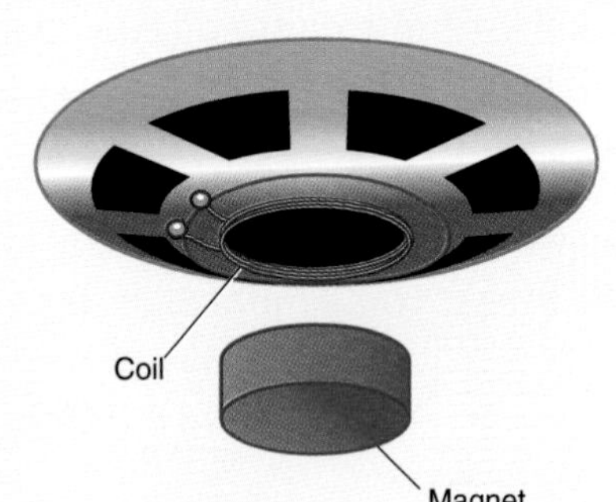

REFLECTING ON THE ACTIVITY AND THE CHALLENGE

You have made a speaker and a microphone. You have learned that a speaker contains a coil of wire with a magnet very close by. When the electric charge from the radio flowed through this coil, the coil vibrated and made sound. A solar cell is able to convert light into electricity. By varying the amount of light, you were able to change the current and make a sound.

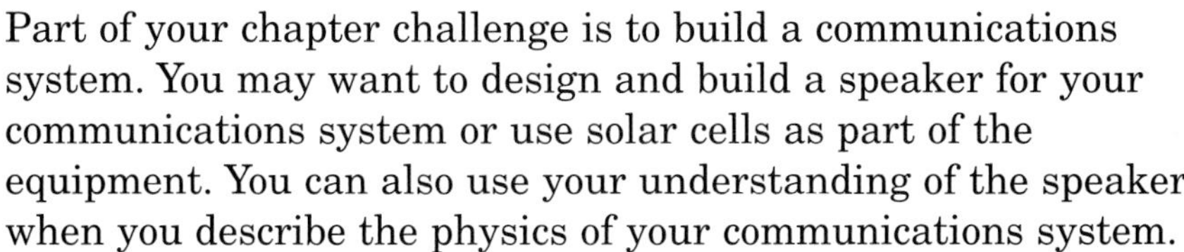

Part of your chapter challenge is to build a communications system. You may want to design and build a speaker for your communications system or use solar cells as part of the equipment. You can also use your understanding of the speaker when you describe the physics of your communications system.

PHYSICS TO GO

1. a) When you plugged the wires from your cup into the personal stereo, what kind of energy entered the cup through the wires?
   b) When you spoke into the cup and heard your voice on the amplifier/speaker, what kind of energy left the cup?

2. How well would your earphone have worked if you only had a 0.1-m wire to wind into a coil (instead of a 1-m wire)? Give a reason for your answer.

3. a) What are the variables that affect the performance of the earphone you built?
   b) If you had whatever materials you wanted and plenty of time, how could you improve the performance of the earphone you built?

4. a) How can a magnet and a coil of wire produce a current?
   b) How can a current and a coil of wire make a magnet?
   c) Use your answer to either part (a) or (b) to explain how a speaker works.
   d) Use your answer to either part (a) or (b) to explain how a microphone works.

5. a) In the activity, you aimed the solar cell at the room lights. If they were fluorescent, you probably heard a hum. What can you conclude about the light that comes from the fluorescent tube?
   b) When you kept the flashlight beam aimed at the solar cell, what did you hear?
   c) What can you conclude about the light that comes from the flashlight?

6. a) Think of the solar cell as a device that transforms energy. What kind of energy was the input energy?
   b) What kind of energy was the output energy?

7. a) Imagine you have a laser instead of the flashlight. How would you set up a communications system like the one in this activity?
   b) Which light source—a laser, a flashlight, or a bulb and convex lens—would enable you to communicate over the greatest distance? Give a reason for your answer.

STRETCHING EXERCISES

1. Take apart an old loudspeaker. Report to the class on what you find inside.

2. Feed the output of the solar cell to an oscilloscope. Observe the wave form for various light sources.

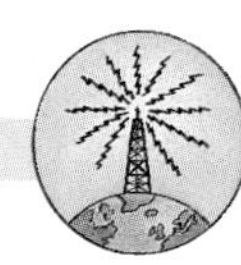

Activity Six

Sending a Message with Light

WHAT DO YOU THINK?

Before long, local telephone lines will be made of tiny glass fibers, and the telephone signals will be sent on light beams. Light has a very high frequency and a short wavelength.

- **How might these properties be important in sending messages?**

Record your ideas about this question in your *Active Physics log*. Be prepared to discuss your responses with your small group and with your class.

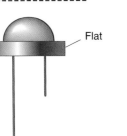

FOR YOU TO DO

1. Obtain an LED, as shown in the diagram. Note that one of the wires from the LED is longer than the other. Also, notice that part of the LED base is flat, not curved. This flat part is next to the shorter wire.

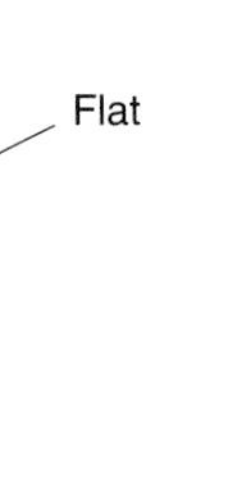

2. Connect the positive side of a battery to the long lead of the LED. If you have wires with alligator clips on each end, you can make this connection with one of those wires. Otherwise, twist the leads together.

3. Obtain a resistor. It is a cylinder with four colored bands. You can connect the resistor in either direction. Connect one end of the resistor to the short lead of the LED. Use a lead with two alligator clips, if you have them.

4. Touch the other end of the resistor to the negative side of the battery. What happens?

   a) Record your observations.

   b) Reverse the battery connections. What happens now?

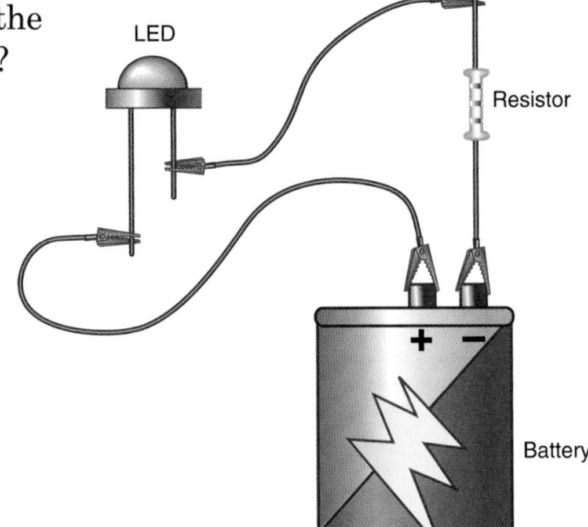

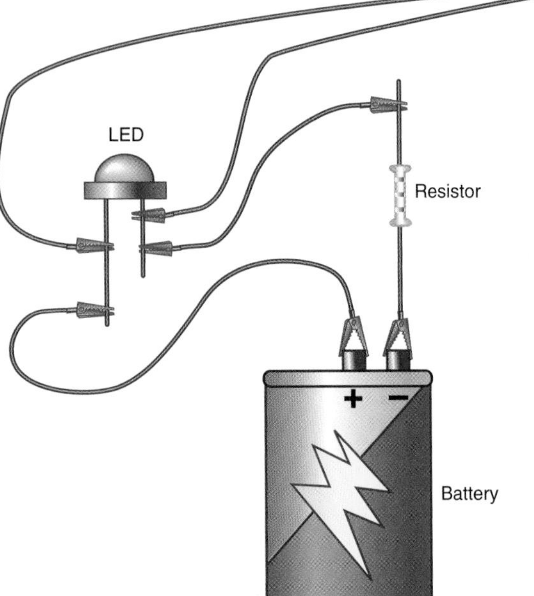

5. Set up the circuit as it was in the first part of step 4. Connect the wires from the plug to the LED leads, as shown. If you do not have wires with alligator clips, *carefully* solder the connections in the circuit. Tape the electrical connections to keep them from touching each other.

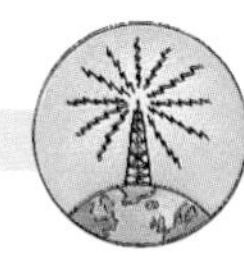

6. Tune the radio to a station. Insert the earphone plug into the earphone jack of the radio.

7. Find a solar cell, with wires to a plug. Turn on the amplifier/speaker. Insert the solar cell plug into the amplifier/speaker's input jack. You will use this circuit as a receiver.

8. The circuit with the LED, which you completed in step 5, will be the transmitter. Point the LED at the solar cell. Move them close together.
   a) With the radio on, what do you hear?
   b) How would you describe the sound quality?

9. Predict what will happen if you place a file card between the LED and the solar cell.
   a) Record your prediction.
   b) Now try it. What happened?
   c) From your observations what can you conclude about how the signal is transmitted from the LED to the solar cell.

10. Increase the separation between the solar cell and the LED.
    a) What happens to the quality of the transmission?

REFLECTING ON THE ACTIVITY AND THE CHALLENGE

You have transmitted music by converting an electrical signal in a wire into light. The LED made the light. When this light reached the solar cell, the solar cell makes another electrical signal. When the speaker/amplifier amplified this signal, you could hear it. If you could shine a beam of light over a long distance, you could use this system for communication. Think of how you might build a communications system with a light source and a solar cell to meet the chapter challenge.

PHYSICS TO GO

1. When you transmitted music in this activity, energy changed forms several times. List each change and where it occurred. Hint: When the music is recorded, the microphones change sound energy into electrical energy.

2. a) Compare what you did in this activity with what you did in Activity Four when you built a telegraph. Which method would you choose to transmit a "yes" or "no" answer? Why?
   b) Which method would you choose to transmit a speech? Why?
   c) Which method would you choose to transmit a simple message 10 m? Why?

3. a) Identify some of the problems with the music transmitter that you built in this activity.
   b) Tell how you might solve these problems. Assume you can get whatever materials you need.

4. a) What effect do you think the room light had on your transmission system?
   b) How could you reduce the effect of room light?

5. a) Do you think the solar cell is designed for bright light or dim light? Explain your answer.
   b) Compared to sunlight, is the light from the LED bright or dim?
   c) Do you think the solar cell is well-matched to the LED? Explain your answer.

6. How could you include a laser in your music-transmission system?

STRETCHING EXERCISE

Obtain a length of optical fiber. Set up the transmission system you built in this activity, but keep the LED away from the solar cell. Put one end of the optical fiber up against the LED and the other end up against the solar cell. Report to the class on how you transmitted music through the optical fiber.

Activity Seven

Just the Fax

WHAT DO YOU THINK?

A fax is a picture sent by telephone. Faxes are remarkably detailed. If you drew a thin line across a page, a typical fax would represent each centimeter of that line by 100 tiny dots.

- **How does the fax machine store and send all the information for each picture?**

Record your ideas about this question in your *Active Physics log*. Be prepared to discuss your responses with your small group and with your class.

FOR YOU TO DO

1. Look at the data shown. It is a stream of zeroes and ones. These numbers are the code for an image. The image is made up of tiny squares. For each square on the image, a one tells that the square is darkened, a zero indicates that the square is light. A coordinate system enables you to match the ones and zeroes to their location in the image.

```
000000001100000110000101001100000000000000000000000111
0001100010100100000000000000000001111000010000100010100
100000000000000000000111101100011011010010000000000000
```

```
000000011111111111101101011000011100000000011111111
111111111111111111100000000000000011111111111111111
111100000000000000000111111110000000000000011111111100000
```

```
011110111111000000000000000111111110000000000011111111
000000000000000111111100000000000001111110000000000000000
0001111111110000000000011110000000000000000000011111110000
```

```
011111111110001100000000000000111111100000000000111101
111100000000000000111111110000000001111000000100011110
00011100110000001111111111001100000000000110011100011000
```

```
111100111110011110000011101001111000110000000111111100
00010000111100001111100011000001111111000010001001110
000111111001110001001111000010000100011000011111110011
```

```
0110011111000100000000001000111111111000110011011111
10000001000000111111110010011011001110011000000100000
111111111100100001001110000100000111110011111110010000
```

```
001001111000001101111111001111111101100001000111111
001111111100101111111010000000000011011110010011111100001
111111001000000000100011100010111000000111111110011000
```

```
00001000011000011111111111111111111100000000000000011110
00000000000011111110110000000000001111110000000001111
111110011100000000001111011000011111111111111100110000
```

```
00000111111000101100111111111101100000000000011111100
000000011111111110011000000000111111110000000000111111
1110100010000000111111111111101100111111111001100000000
```

```
1111111111110101111111111111001000000000111111111111
0101001111111111001000000000111111111111101010011111111
1111000000000011111111111110101001111111111111000000000
```

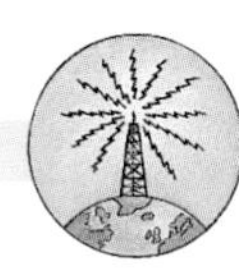

2. On a piece of graph paper, write the numbers 1 to 40 across the top, and the numbers 1 to 40 down the left side, as shown.

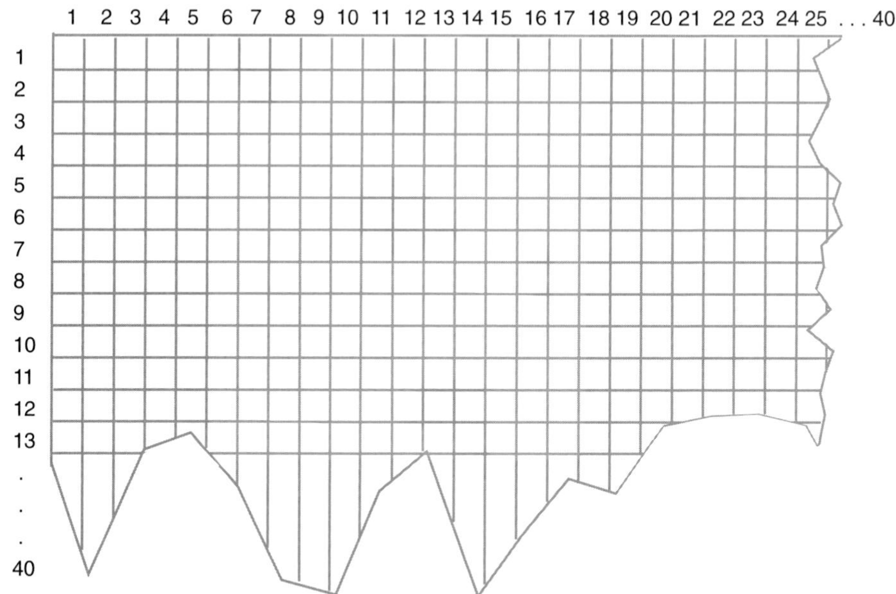

3. Now translate the data you are assigned onto your graph paper. As you begin reading ones and zeroes from the top left, move across the first row of the data from the top left to the top right. When you reach the right side of a row of data, drop down to the next row and begin reading again from left to right. When you reach the right side of the row on the graph paper, drop down to the second row of graph paper and keep on going. Rows of data do not correspond to rows of the graph paper.
   a) Record the data on your graph paper.

4. Your teacher will assign each group a section of the image. Within your group, decide how to prepare your part of the image. When you are done, cut out your group's part of the image and glue it to the "master" image that your teacher will give you.

5. Look at the finished image from a distance. The white and dark squares on the graph paper are called *pixels*.
   a) In your log record what you see. Where have you seen this picture before?

6. Look at the picture below. Hold this picture at reading distance.

a) Record what you see.
b) Step back several paces. How is what you see different from what you saw in part (a).
c) Write a brief explanation in your log of what happened. Be sure to discuss what happened to the pixels.

7. Examine the fax through your magnifier.

a) How many pixels high is the fax image?
b) How many pixels wide is the fax image?
c) What is the total number of pixels in the fax image?

8. Examine a newspaper photograph.

a) How is it similar to a fax?
b) How is it different from a fax?
c) Estimate the number of dots in a typical newspaper photograph.

REFLECTING ON THE ACTIVITY AND THE CHALLENGE

You now understand that data sent over telephone lines is a series of ones and zeroes. Each one or zero describes one pixel of the image. You also understand that when you look at the fax picture close-up, you see the individual pixels. When you back away, the individual pixels disappear and you see the image as a whole. This set of data can be sent over a telephone line to transmit a picture. To meet the chapter challenge, you might want to send a picture. You can use what you have learned in the other activities to send a series of ones and zeroes. The pattern of pixels you construct from could be in a code that contains the message.

PHYSICS TO GO

1. How large is the pixel size for a typical fax? Hint: See What Do You Think? in this activity.

2. a) Look at a computer screen or TV screen. Use a magnifier to get a good view. Describe what you see.
   b) Compare what you see to what you see when you look at a fax through a magnifier.

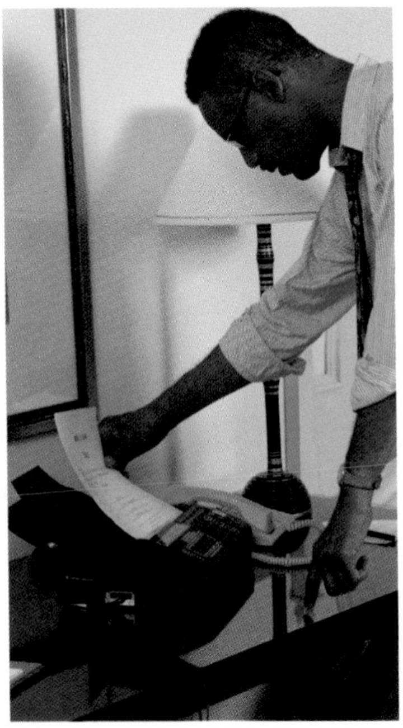

3. A fax of a page of text requires approximately 30 s to transmit. Estimate the amount of dots which must be sent in the page of text by counting the number of lines of information and the number of dots horizontally and vertically in each letter. Calculate the transmission rate of the fax.

4. Compare Morse code to a fax.

5. Japanese is a different language than English. Why was the fax so important for transmitting information in Japanese? Hint: You may need to look up information about how Japanese is written.

6. How are pictures sent back to Earth from space?

7. A small fax machine has only ten pixels in each row. On a piece of graph paper, create the image from the data stream below. Rows of data do not correspond to rows of the fax.

```
0000000000001001000000100
100000011111100000011010
0000111010000010101000001
0100000001010000000000000
```

8. The image you make in this activity had only two kinds of pixels—white or black. Making pixels in shades of gray can increase the detail shown in the image. If you could use five different shades (white, three shades of gray, and black), how many ones and zeroes would you need to transmit the picture?

STRETCHING EXERCISES

1. Look at a newspaper photograph and a black-and-white photographic print through a microscope. Research the concept of "grain" in a photographic print. Use your research to understand what you see in the microscope. Report to the class on what you find.

2. Research the painter Georges Seurat. Find out how Seurat's painting is related to the fax and newspaper pictures that you studied in this activity.

Activity Eight
Bar Codes

WHAT DO YOU THINK?

A bar code mail sorter can read 30,000 envelope addresses per hour.

- **How does the red light scan products you buy?**
- **How does the bar code work?**

Record your ideas about these questions in your *Active Physics log*. Be prepared to discuss your responses with your small group and with your class.

FOR YOU TO DO

1. Look at the postal bar code.

a) What does the bar code consist of?

10010/2007 

Example
7 4 2 1 0

4+2=6

2. The bars are organized into groups of five. Each bar location has a value. Reading from left to right in a group, the values are 7, 4, 2, 1 and 0, as shown in the drawing of the bar code key.

   a) In each group of five, how many bars are long, and how many are short?

   b) Look at the representation of the number 6 which is enlarged from the bar code key. The second and third bars are long. They correspond to the values 4 and 2. Since $4 + 2 = 6$, this is the way 6 is represented. What digit is represented by each of the following bar codes?

   c) Draw the bar codes for the digits 2 and 7.

   d) Is there any digit from zero to nine that cannot be represented using the above rules?

   e) If the first two bars are long, the ZIP digit is zero. Make the bar code for the digit zero.

3. Look at a whole zip code. There are nine digits in a ZIP code. But when the ZIP code is translated into a bar code, there are ten bar groups. The first nine groups give the nine digits in the code. The last group of five bars is a check digit. It helps catch any mistakes in either printing or reading the code.

   To find the check digit, you first perform several steps.

   - Add up the first nine digits in the code.
   - Find the next higher multiple of ten.
   - Subtract the sum from the next multiple of ten.
   - The result of the subtraction is the check digit.

   a) What is the check digit for the zip code shown to the left?

Zip Code: 52847-2014

4. The very first bar and the very last bar are not part of the code. These bars are called "frame bits." They show the beginning and the end of the code. Find the frame bits in the code above.

   a) Record in your log how to read a ZIP code.

5. Use what you have learned to "crack the code." Notice that you must separate the bars into groups of five yourself. Remember that the first and last bars are the "frame bits."

a)

b) Write the zip codes for

Nowhere, USA 01234-9876

Somewhere, USA 56789-0001

c) Write the bar code for your birthday.

d) Write the bar code for your height.

REFLECTING ON THE ACTIVITY AND THE CHALLENGE

You have learned how to write a bar code for a number. You have learned how each group of five bars represents one digit and how the bars are read to form a zip code. You could use this code to help meet the chapter challenge. You could send a message with a zip code if you can find a way to transmit the bars from one room to another. Think about how you might do this. If the message was a sentence, you would have to convert each letter to a number.

PHYSICS TO GO

1. a) What is special about the first and last bars in the zip code?
   b) Are the first and last bars long or short?

2. How are zeroes represented by bars in the ZIP code?

3. Write the ZIP code for this bar code.

4. Write the bar code for this zip code: 08420-1670

5. Show how two long bars produce each digit from one to nine. Hint: Use the bar code key. For example, to produce 5, you will add 4 and 1. The long bars would be under the 4 and the 1, and the other bars would be short.

6. The code for zero is made with two bars, but it does not follow the same code as the other eight digits. Why is zero an exception? Hint: Using the bar code key, look for two numbers that add up to zero.

7. Why does using a bar code for the ZIP code make mail sorting easier?

8. a) What information do you think is put on the bar codes at a supermarket?
   b) How is the use of the bar codes helpful in running a supermarket?

STRETCHING EXERCISES

1. A remote control from a TV sends a signal that is like a bar code. The signal is sent with infrared radiation, which is similar to light. We cannot see infrared, but a video camera can record it. Aim a video camera at the TV remote. Shoot a video while someone pushes the remote buttons. The camera responds to the infrared from the remote. What do you see on the video?

2. Explore the effect a magnet has on iron filings. Now put the magnet far away. Sprinkle some filings on a credit card. Gently tap the card to remove the larger filings. Examine the card with a magnifier. What do you see? How do you think information is coded on the card? When you are finished, be sure to gently wipe off all the filings.

3. What type of bar codes are used in supermarkets? Investigate the following:

   How are products coded at the manufacturer?

   How are products coded at the supermarket?

   How do manufacturers and the supermarkets use the bar codes?

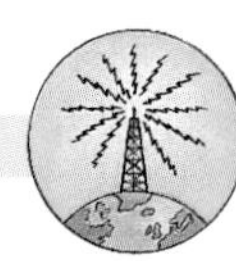

PHYSICS AT WORK

Dale Hatfield

Webster's *New World Dictionary* defines a hobby as "something that one likes to do or study in one's spare time." A career is defined as "a profession or occupation which one trains for and pursues as a lifework." In fact, for Dale Hatfield, the Chief of the Office of Engineering and Technology at the Federal Communications Commission (FCC), his hobby has become his career.

As a child he liked communications technology. "When I was 12 years old I built my own ham radio," says Dale, "and I soon realized there was an important connection between radio technology, math, and science."

At the FCC his most important responsibility is to manage the radio spectrum and decide what frequencies should be used for what purposes. Sounds easy enough until you realize just how many things need their own radio frequency. There are radio stations, television stations, amateur radio stations, police and fire departments, airports, and satellites. There are also cellular phones, pagers, cordless telephones, baby monitors, keyless entry systems, and many other personal devices which necessitate enough frequencies so that their many users do not collide with each other. "You can't have a taxicab on the same frequency as NBC," explains Dale.

"One of the tricks to finding additional space is to use higher and higher frequencies, but at a certain point radio waves begin to work like light waves and reflect off buildings, snow, and rain. They are then no longer effective."

In addition to managing wireless communication, the FCC is responsible for regulating long-distance "wired" communication. The latest and greatest advance in this area is fiber optics. In contrast to traditional phone lines, fiber optic lines are made of glass with a reflective property to keep the light waves intact and traveling without resistance. "A tremendous amount of information can be sent more efficiently through fiber optic lines," Dale explains, "and the technology is still advancing."

As technology continues to advance, so does the need for lifelong experts like Dale Hatfield. In 1997, after 18 years of service with the United States government, Dale was thinking about retiring. But the FCC offered him his current position and "it sounded like fun" so he took it and has not looked back. Why retire when your life's work is your favorite pastime?

Chapter 2 Assessment

1. Now that you have completed this chapter, you are ready to engineer a communication system. You and your team may already have a good idea of the type of system you wish to develop, and the type of message you wish to send.

   During the test of your system, you must measure the speed of transmission of your system. After a successful test, each team member will submit a written report about the system. This report will have the following parts:

   a) the design of the system
   b) how your method of communication is better for this challenge than the other methods you investigated in this chapter
   c) the physics of your system
   d) your measurement of the speed of transmission in words per minute, symbols per minute, or notes per minute.

2. Some of the activities in this chapter also focused on privacy and confidentiality in a communication system.
   You can now write an essay about the stealing of information on the Internet.

   Or, perhaps you have formed opinions about restricting Internet access to young children, and may wish to write an essay about that.

   Review the criteria you and your classmates established at the beginning of the chapter for grading your work. Now that you have completed the chapter you may wish to make additional alterations to the suggested scheme.

A grade will be assigned to the speed and quality of the transmission. 40 points

The quality of your written report will also be graded: 60 points

a) explanation of design (including drawings) 15 points
b) how your method is better than others 15 points
c) the physics of your system 25 points
d) your measurement of the speed of transmission of your system 5 points

You may also wish to develop a detailed grading scheme for your essay.

Physics You Learned

An electric current can produce magnetism.

A moving magnet can produce electricity.

The current and number of turns are important variables in the electromagnet.

A speaker contains a moving coil and a magnet.

A telegraph contains an electromagnet.

Light can be transformed into electricity.

Electricity can be transformed into light.

Messages can be sent with spring waves, a tight string, light, and electricity.

A series of ones and zeroes can be a code for an image.

A series of bars can be a code for a digit.

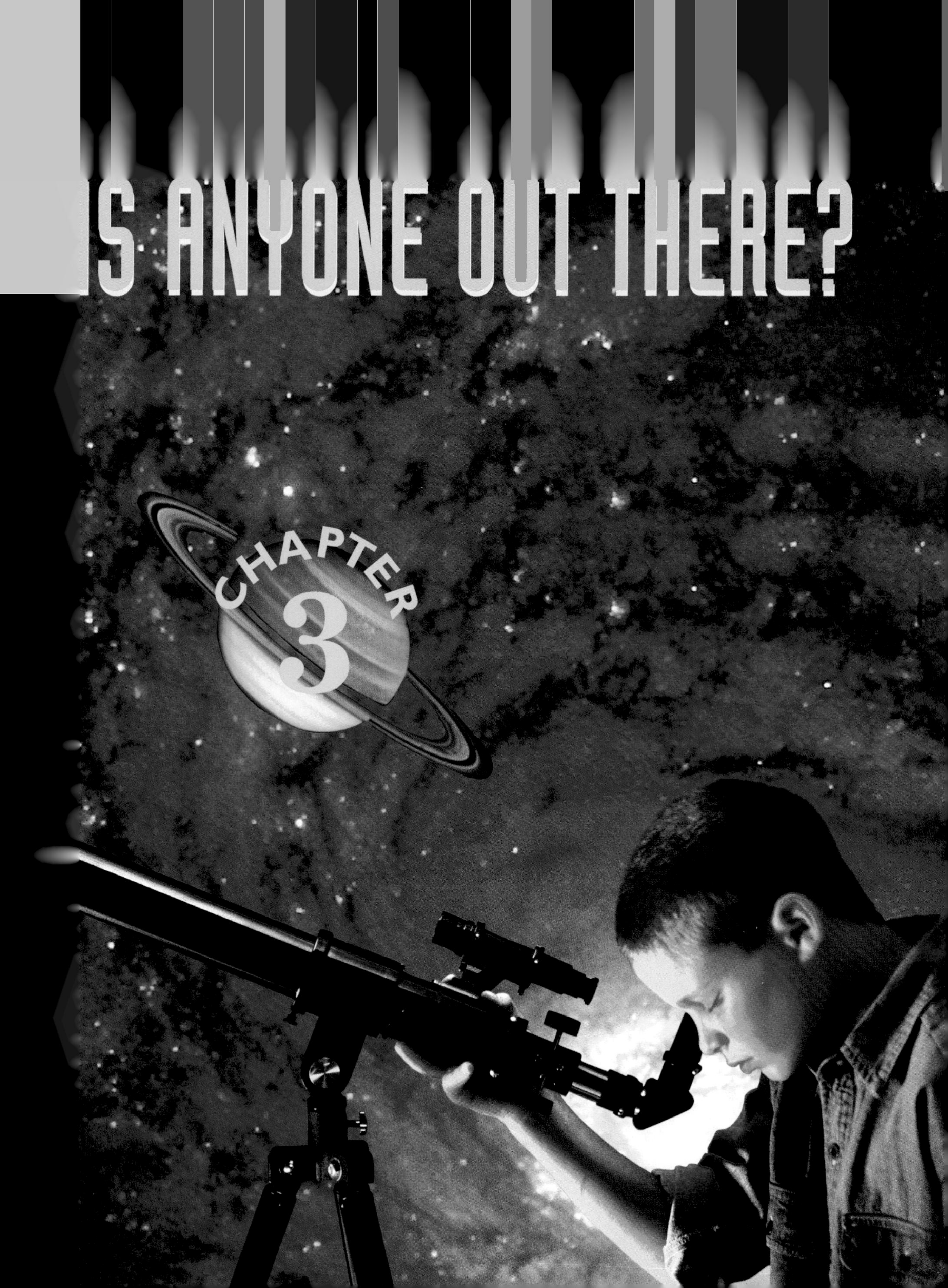
IS ANYONE OUT THERE?
CHAPTER
3

Scenario

Science has provided you with an enormous amount of knowledge about the world. Most of that knowledge has come from direct experience with objects that you can hold in your hands. You do experiments in a laboratory. Science experiments are also conducted on land, in the oceans, in the air and in space. Since these experiments are designed to test ideas about how things work, scientists have developed a relatively good understanding of the Earth and the life on it.

By comparison, almost nothing is known about life outside the Earth. Scientists estimate that there should be a huge number of planets with conditions that can support life. These planets would have about the same range of temperatures and the same kind of atmosphere as Earth. Throughout the universe, there ought to be millions of possible locations for life to evolve. But if there is life out there, it may not be very advanced. And even if it were advanced, how would it be possible to communicate over such tremendous distances?

Some scientists have dedicated their life's work to the effort of finding extraterrestrial life. They have identified stars that might have planets with conditions similar to Earth. They observe the sky closely for possible signals from advanced civilizations. When they think about communication with other life forms, they use both science and language. The search for extraterrestrial life is expensive. Is it sensible to fund this type of research?

Challenge

1. Outline a plan to look for and listen for extraterrestrial life. Develop methods that are based on sound scientific principles. In this part of the challenge, you will show *how* you would communicate with any life forms you discover.

2. Decide *what* to say to extraterrestrial beings. Remember that you might make contact with a civilization that is more or less technologically advanced than that on Earth. Certainly they will not speak English. The message must:
   - use science and mathematics that the extraterrestrial beings can understand, and
   - present important information about human life and the Earth.
3. Write an essay describing what could be learned from contact with extraterrestrial beings.
4. Hold a mock hearing of the Space Committee of the United States Senate. Some of the students will be senators. Some will be scientists who would like to begin a search for extraterrestrial life. The scientists are requesting $3 billion for the project. They must convince the Senate Committee that the money will be well spent. Many of the Committee members are skeptical, so the scientists must be persuasive.

Assessment

Most of your grade will be based on how well you apply the physics you will learn in this chapter to the challenge. Part of your grade will be determined by your imagination and creativity.

As a class discuss the questions below as you develop your grading system for this challenge.

- Should you do every part of the challenge? Or, should you select one or two of the parts?
- How can you assess your creativity?

When you have answered these two questions, you can create the grading system. Here is an example of one way to grade the first two parts of the challenge:

Part 1:

Choice of methods to communicate: 40 points

Explanation of the science:

correct statement of science concepts: 25 points

how Chapter 3 activities present these concepts: 35 points

Part 2:

Choice of language for communication; discussion of how extraterrestrials will be able to understand the science:

correct statement of science used in communication: 25 points

how extraterrestrials might use the science in a message: 25 points

Choice of message content: 25 points

Description of how the content is important: 25 points

Activity One

Lenses and Ray Optics

WHAT DO YOU THINK?

- **What do a camera, photocopier, and slide projector have in common?**
- **How do they function?**

Record your ideas about these questions in your *Active Physics log*. Be prepared to discuss your responses with your small group and with your class.

FOR YOU TO DO

1. A convex (or converging) lens is thicker in the middle and thinner at the edges, as shown. Use a convex lens, a bright light bulb, and a white screen to simulate a photocopier. Move the lens and the screen until the image of the bulb is sharp, and the same size as the actual bulb. An image on a screen is called a *real image*.

a) Describe what you see.

b) Measure and record the distance of the bulb (object) from the lens and the image from the lens.

Do not use lenses with chipped edges. Mount lenses securely in a holder.

2. Use the convex lens, bulb, and screen to construct a simulation of a slide projector. Make the image twice the size of the object.

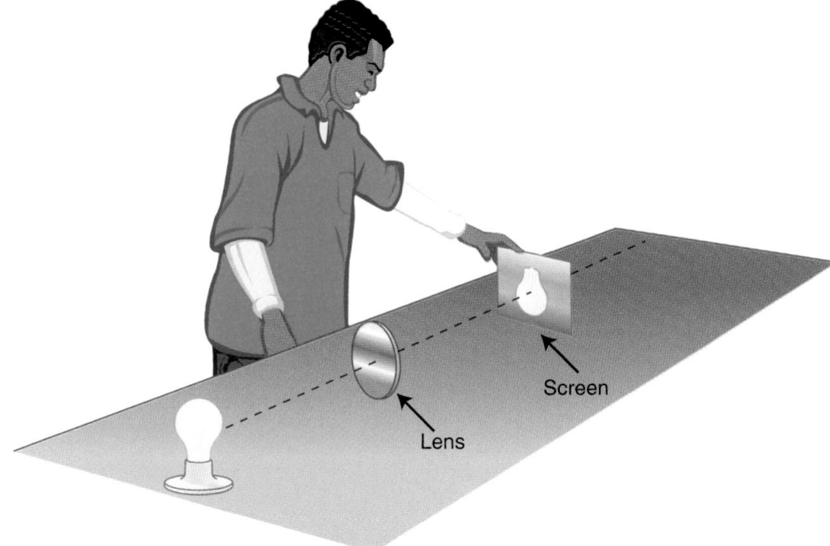

a) Measure and record the distance of the object from the lens and the image from the lens.

3. Use the lens, bulb, and screen to simulate a camera. Make the image size one-quarter the size of the object.

a) Measure and record the distance of the object from the lens and the image.

4. Obtain a second convex lens, and repeat step 1.
   a) Measure and record the distance of the object from the lens and the image from the lens for the second convex lens.
   b) How do these distances compare with those you measured in step 1?
   c) What do you think makes one convex lens different from another?

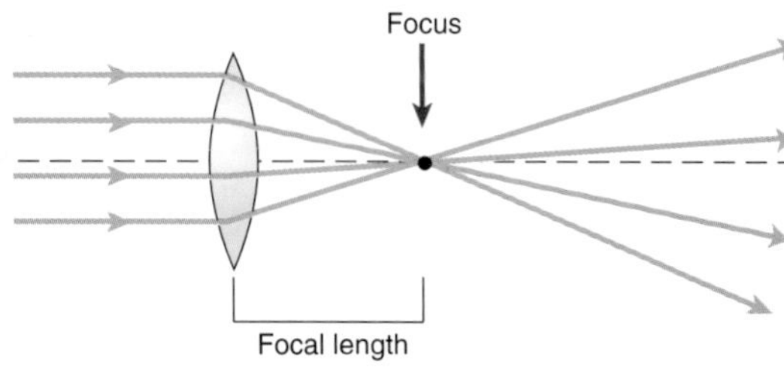

5. Use the first convex lens. Measure the image distance when the object is very far away, like a tree outside the lab window.
   a) Record this distance.
   b) Repeat step 5 for a second convex lens. Record this distance.
   c) The distance between the lens and the image of a distant object is called the *focal length*. The position of the image is at the *focus* of the lens, as shown. From your results of parts (a) and (b), give the focal length of each lens.
   d) How does the focal length of each lens compare with the image distance you found in steps 1 and 4 (image size equals object size)?

6. Look directly through each convex lens at a distant object and through each convex lens at an object only a few centimeters away.
   a) Record what you see in each case.
   b) How is what you saw with each lens different?
   c) How does the magnifying power of each lens compare with its focal length? Write a general statement about the relationship between the focal length and how much the convex lens magnifies.

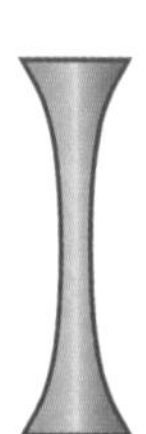

7. A concave lens is thinner in the middle and thicker at the edges, as shown. Using a concave lens and a bright light bulb try to make an image on a white screen.
   a) Could you make an image on the screen?

8. Look directly through the concave lens at a variety of objects around you.
   a) Record what you see.
   b) How is what you saw with the concave lens different from what you saw using the convex lens?

PHYSICS TALK

These are the equations that describe relationships in a convex lens.

$$\frac{1}{f} = \frac{1}{D_o} + \frac{1}{D_i}$$

$$\frac{S_o}{S_i} = \frac{D_o}{D_i}$$

where f is the focal length of the lens
D_o is the object distance
D_i is the image distance
S_o is the object size
S_i is the image size

If the rays of light actually converge to a point, the image

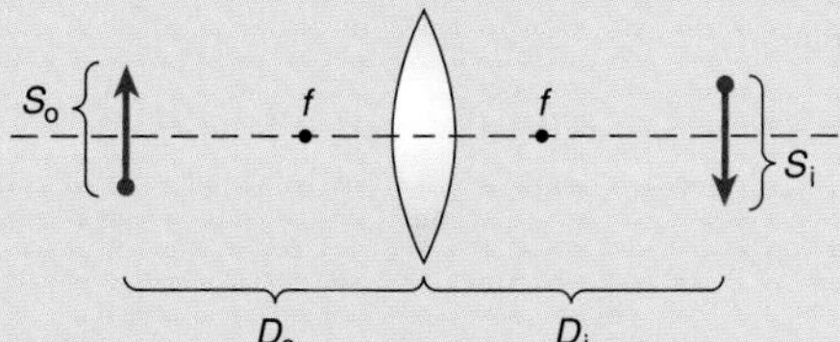

is a *real image*. A real image can be projected on a screen. If the light only appears to come together, the image is a *virtual image* and cannot be projected on a screen.

REFLECTING ON THE ACTIVITY AND THE CHALLENGE

You have learned that a convex lens makes an image on a screen and can be used as a magnifying glass. You have also learned that concave lenses cannot form an image on a screen and do not magnify. Also, you have learned about the focal length, which is a most important property of a lens. To meet the chapter challenge, you must make a plan to look and listen for life in space. Your plan can include observations made through telescopes, and your understanding of lenses is essential to understanding how the telescope works. Your next activity will deal with telescopes.

PHYSICS TO GO

1. a) Copy the drawing on your paper.

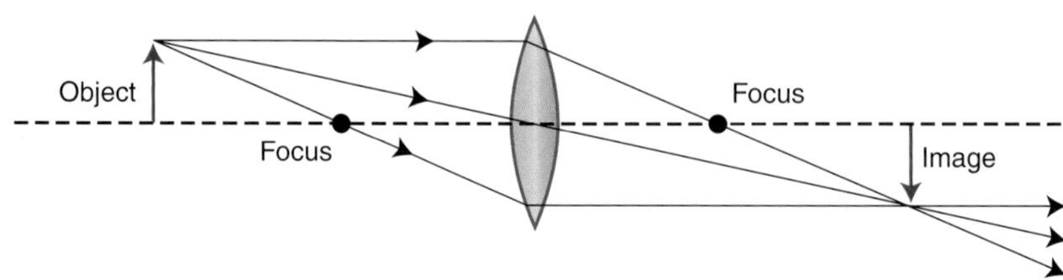

b) Label the object distance and the image distance.
c) If you move the object further away from the lens, what happens to the image distance?
d) If you move the object closer to the lens, what happens to the image distance?

2. Many optical devices use lenses. For the devices listed below, describe the object and the image. Estimate the object distance and the image distance. Also, estimate the object size and the image size.
   a) slide projector
   b) camera
   c) telescope
   d) photocopy machine
   e) the human eye
   f) magnifying glass

3. a) Your lab partner holds a bright light at night. You set up a convex lens and a white screen to make a sharp image of the light. Now your lab partner begins to walk away from you. What must you do to keep the image sharp?
   b) Now your lab partner begins to walk towards you. What must you do to keep the image sharp?

4. For each of the optical devices listed in question 2 above, tell whether the image is real or virtual and if real, the location of the "screen."

5. a) Give an example of how a convex lens makes a real image.
   b) Give an example of how a convex lens makes a virtual image.
   c) Give an example of how a concave lens makes a virtual image.

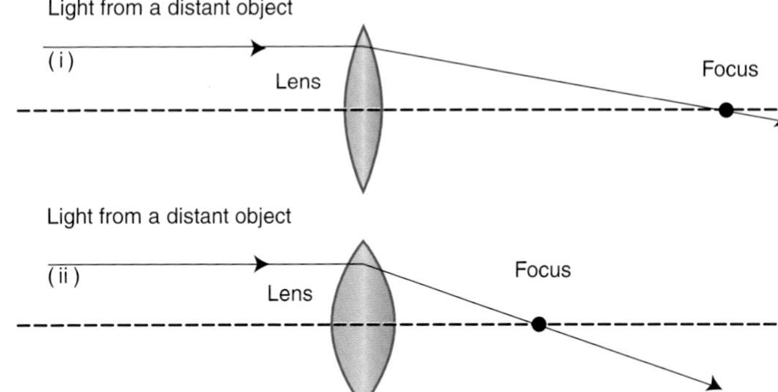

6. a) Tell how to measure the focal length of a lens.
   b) If you had two lenses with different focal lengths, which would make the stronger magnifier?
   c) Look at the two drawings of lens (i) and lens (ii). Which lens has the shorter focal length? How could you tell?

7. A convex lens with a focal length of 0.05 m makes an image that is 3 m away from the lens. Where is the object?

8. a) If the distance from the image to the convex lens and the distance from the object to the convex lens are both 0.2 m, what is the focal length of the lens?
   b) Suppose the image and object are both the same distance from the convex lens. Make a general statement about how this distance is related to the focal length.

9. a) A convex lens has a focal length of 0.08 m. Where is the image of an object that is 1 m away?
   b) Where is the image of an object that is 5 m away?
   c) Where is the image of an object that is 20 m away?
   d) If the object is extremely far from the lens, how is the focal length related to the image distance?
   e) Show how the equation in Physics Talk predicts your answer to part (d).

STRETCHING EXERCISE

Find a convex lens and measure its focal length. Now make an image of a light bulb on a screen. Investigate how the image distance changes as you change the object distance. Make a graph of the object distance and the image distance. See if your results agree with the prediction of the lens equation given in Physics Talk.

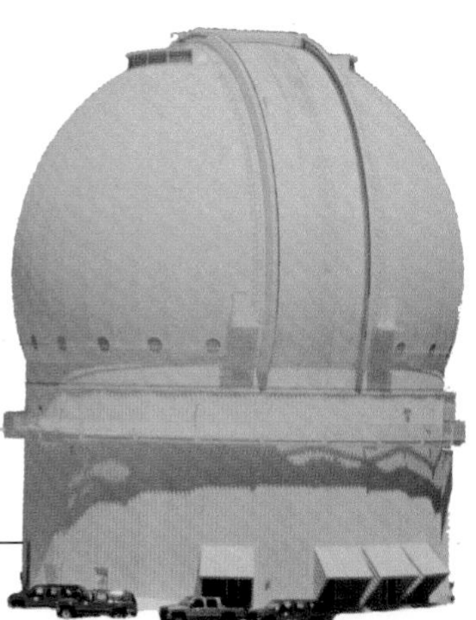

Activity Two

The Telescope

WHAT DO YOU THINK?

One of Einstein's most famous predictions was that light can be bent by gravity. Astronomers tested this idea during an eclipse of the sun. They aimed their telescope at stars right at the edge of the sun. The positions of the stars were shifted just as Einstein predicted they would be.

- **How does a telescope work?**
- **How could a telescope be improved?**

Record your ideas about these questions in your *Active Physics log*. Be prepared to discuss your responses with your small group and with your class.

FOR YOU TO DO

1. Obtain two convex lenses. One with a very small focal length, and one with a much longer focal length. Measure the focal length of each lens.

   a) Record the focal length of each lens in your log.

2. Mount the lens with the shorter focal length on one end of a meter stick. When you use the telescope you will assemble, you will look through this lens. It is called the eyepiece.

3. The other lens is called the objective. To find out where to place the objective lens, add the two focal lengths that you measured in step 1. This sum is the distance between the two lenses. When you have found this distance, mount the objective, as shown in the diagram.

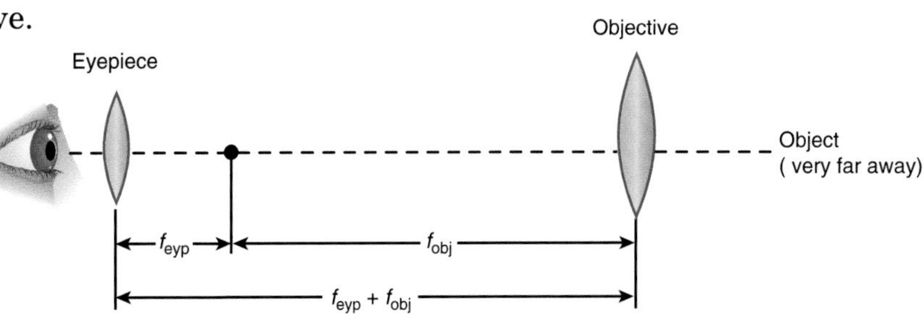

a) In your log, make a drawing similar to the one shown. Label the distance between the two lenses.

4. Observe a distant object outside. Be sure that light from this object travels through both lenses to your eye.

a) What do you see? Make a drawing for your log.

b) Record how the object appeared through your telescope.

5. An astronomical telescope magnifies objects. The objects look larger through the telescope than they do through the "naked eye." The magnification M tells how much larger the object appears. M is simply the ratio of the two focal lengths:

$$M = \frac{f_{obj}}{f_{eyp}}$$

where f_{obj} = focal length of the objective lens

f_{eyp} = focal length of the eyepiece

a) Using the focal lengths of the two lenses in your telescope, predict the magnification.

6. Obtain two other lenses that will give a different magnification. Measure their focal lengths.

a) Record the focal lengths in your log.

b) Calculate the magnification for these two lenses.

c) Predict how what you see through these lenses will be different from what you saw in step 4. Record your prediction.

7. Set up the two lenses as you did in step 3. Observe a distant object.
   a) Record how the object appears through this telescope. Make a drawing for your log.
   b) Compare the results with those you obtained in step 4, and with the prediction you made in step 6. How do the results compare with your prediction?

FOR YOU TO READ

Refracting and Reflecting Telescopes

You have made a simple *refracting* telescope. In a refractor, the light enters the telescope through the objective lens. The focal length of this lens is an important characteristic of the telescope. The longer the focal length, the larger the image. A telescope that observes details of the surfaces of planets, or that measures the parallax of nearby stars, has an objective with a very long focal length. The focal length of the objective lens of the refractor at Yerkes Observatory is 18 m. Imagine building a mount to aim a telescope that long!

Unfortunately, in a large image, the light is spread out so much that the image becomes very dim. To make a brighter image requires more light. That means the objective lens must be larger in diameter, to let in more light. The refractor at the Yerkes Observatory has a diameter of about 1.0 m. Imagine making a lens that large!

The difficulty of making large lenses led to the need for the *reflecting* telescope. In a reflector, a large concave mirror makes an image. The astronomer observes the image through an eyepiece lens. Modern astronomical telescopes are reflectors.

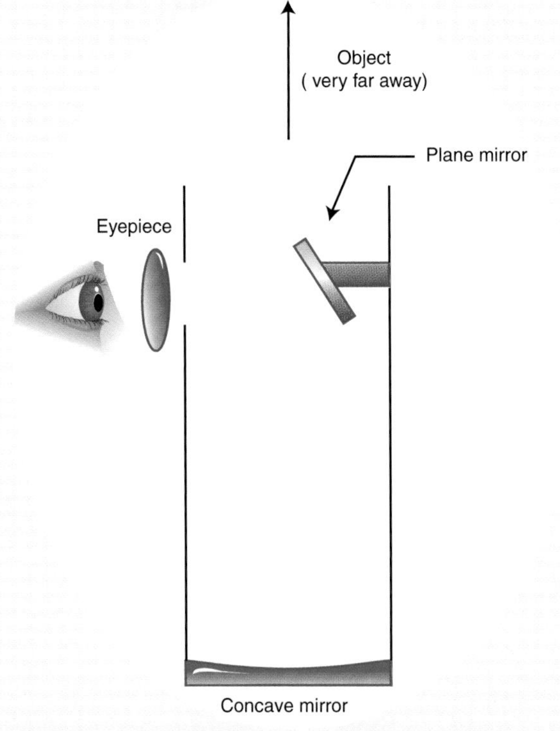

REFLECTING ON THE ACTIVITY AND THE CHALLENGE

You have learned how to make a telescope. You have seen that a telescope contains two lenses, and that the focal length of the objective is much longer than the focal length of the eyepiece. You have learned that it is essential to line up these lenses carefully, so both point right at the object. You can use what you have learned to meet the chapter challenge, since one way to look for life in space is to look through telescopes. From your work in this activity, you will be able to explain and demonstrate how a telescope works.

PHYSICS TO GO

1. Describe the lenses that can be used to make a telescope.

2. a) You are observing a distant light bulb through your telescope. If you held a card between the eyepiece and objective, could you make an image of the light bulb on the card?
   b) Where would this image appear?
   c) You look at this image through a convex eyepiece. Then you switch to a concave eyepiece. Which eyepiece would give the larger image? Why?

3. a) The longer the focal length of the objective, the greater the magnification. If the focal length of the objective increases, what happens to the length of the telescope? Explain your answer.
   b) If you wanted to increase the magnification of a telescope, why couldn't you simply get an objective lens with a much longer focal length and make the telescope much longer? What would happen if you did? Hint: The real image from the objective lens will be much larger. But the same amount of light will be spread over a much larger image.

4. Explain how a telescope lets you see a magnified image.

5. a) How is the diameter of the objective lens important in a telescope?
   b) The Mt. Palomar telescope has a mirror to collect the light. The mirror is 200 inches across. Why are telescopes made with such large openings?

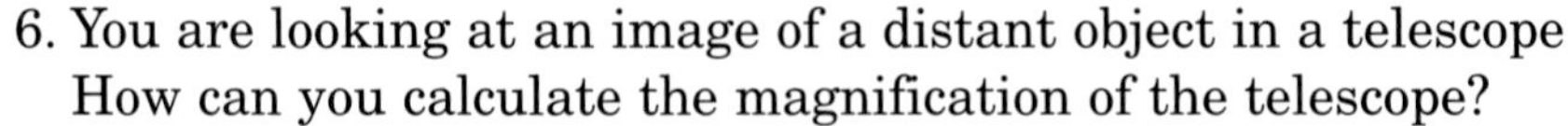

6. You are looking at an image of a distant object in a telescope. How can you calculate the magnification of the telescope?

7. a) In old pirate movies, the captain of the ship would take a small device out of his pocket and pull on the ends to make it longer. Then the captain would use this device to view distant objects. What is this device?

   b) How does it work?

   c) Draw a diagram of what you think is inside.

8. Write an advertisement to sell telescopes in the 1600s.

9. Part of the search for extraterrestrial life is the search for planets that could support life. Planets, like Earth, shine only with reflected light, so they are not very bright. Also, they are usually small. A planet moving around a star would probably be lost in all the light the star gives off. But as the planet circles the star, it pulls the star itself back and forth. In 1995 astronomers observed this kind of back-and-forth motion of a star. They concluded that the star had a planet! Since then, many more stars with planets have been identified. Discuss how these observations might aid the search for extraterrestrial life.

STRETCHING EXERCISE

1. Different kinds of telescopes can be used in observing "invisible" signals, such as ultraviolet, infrared, microwave, and radio waves. Research one of these devices to learn what information they provide.

2. Research the Hubble Space Telescope. You can get plenty of information at the NASA site on the world-wide web.
   - Find out why the Hubble is more capable than ground-based telescopes.
   - Describe some important discoveries that have been made with the Hubble telescope.

Activity Three

Digital Imaging

WHAT DO YOU THINK?

The digital sound of the CD revolutionized the audio recording industry. The digital picture of High Density Television (HDTV) is about to revolutionize the television industry.

- **What is analog?**
- **What is digital?**
- **How does each work?**

Record your ideas about these questions in your *Active Physics log*. Be prepared to discuss your responses with your small group and with your class.

FOR YOU TO DO

1. The “3” in the diagram is represented by a pattern of pixels. The pattern is nine pixels high by five pixels wide.

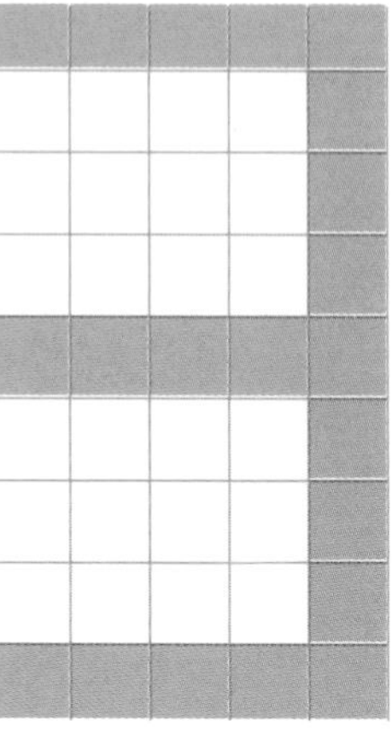

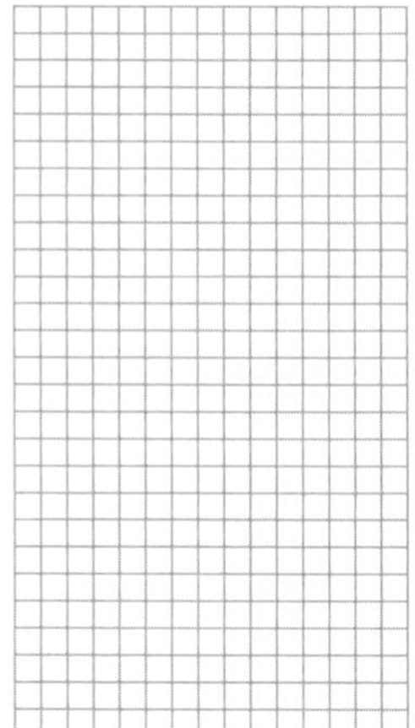

a) On graph paper, make similar pixel patterns to represent the other numbers from zero to nine.

b) On a piece of graph paper, repeat part (a) but with more pixels in the same space. Make the pixels smaller, so you have 27 pixels high and 15 pixels wide. Notice that the total area of the pixels is the same as in part (a), where the pattern was 9 pixels high by 5 pixels wide.

c) If you had more pixels available, how would that affect the quality of the figure? Explain why.

2. You are an engineer who has to design a way to represent numbers from zero to nine. Your display must contain as few pixels as possible, but it still must be easy-to-read.

a) What is the minimum number of pixels you can use? Explain how you found your answer.

Digital Representation

```
1 1 1 1 1
0 0 0 0 1
0 0 0 0 1
0 0 0 0 1
1 1 1 1 1
0 0 0 0 1
0 0 0 0 1
0 0 0 0 1
1 1 1 1 1
```

3. You can use the numbers one and zero to represent numbers, in the same way you used pixels above. A one means the pixel is on, so the pixel is black. A zero means the pixel is off, so the pixel is white, like the rest of the page. Look at the “3” made with zeroes and ones. This is called a digital representation.

a) Choose two other one-digit numbers. On a piece of graph paper, represent these numbers digitally (make a picture with zeroes and ones).

b) See if your lab partners can decode your picture and identify the number.

4. Turn on a computer. Examine the screen closely with a magnifier. Pay special attention to numbers and letters.
   a) Describe what you see.
   b) How does the existence of letters complicate the digital representation of numbers?
   c) Could you tell letters apart with an array of nine by five pixels? If not, how many pixels would you need?

5. Examine a newspaper photo with a magnifying glass.
   a) Can you see the individual dots of ink?
   b) Look at the individual dots. How many different levels of light, dark, and gray can you find?
   c) Examine a black-and-white magazine photo with a magnifier. Compare the dots in the newspaper and magazine photos.

FOR YOU TO READ

Digital Images

As you have seen, an image on a computer monitor is made up of tiny lighted dots. Inside the computer, the image is stored digitally. It is stored as a series of ones and zeroes. These numbers tell whether each dot on the monitor screen is lighted or dark. The dots are all arranged on a grid, which is a rectangular coordinate system. This grid covers the whole screen.

A dot matrix printer makes images in the same way. The dot is either printed or it is not. When you see the dots, your eye and brain combine them to make a letter, number, or picture.

A modern telescope also uses pixels. The astronomer sits in front of a computer monitor. The monitor displays a black-and-white image of the stars. Each pixel can typically display eight different levels of brightness.

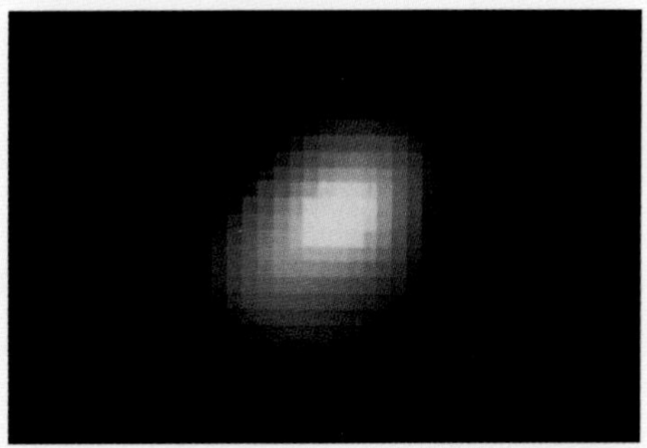

In a color computer monitor, each pixel can light up in different colors. A pixel could be red, blue, green, or any combination of the three. And each of these three colors can be shown in many different levels of brightness. That's why making color computer images uses up so much computer memory.

REFLECTING ON THE ACTIVITY AND THE CHALLENGE

You have learned how digital images are made. You have made numbers with patterns of dots, and you have represented the dots with ones and zeroes. You can use what you have learned to create a message for an extraterrestrial. If your message is a picture, you now know how to represent it in a way that can be stored in a computer.

PHYSICS TO GO

1. a) Examine a black and white print (on photographic paper) with a magnifier. How is this print different from a digital image?

   b) If you scan the print into a computer, you turn it into a digital image. If you printed out the image from the computer, how would it look different from the original print?

   c) Why would some astronomers prefer photographic slides over computer images?

2. a) Suppose you want to buy a printer. A store has two different models. One has 80 dots per centimeter, and the other has 240 dots per centimeter. If the cost and features were similar, which would you choose and why?

   b) Would the extra number of dots per centimeter be more important for representing numbers or letters?

3. a) A standard TV screen has about 400 horizontal lines and about 500 vertical lines. What is the total number of pixels on the screen?

   b) Look at the screen with a magnifying glass. Can you count the lines?

   c) Look at a modern computer video screen with a magnifying glass. Compare the computer image with the TV image.

   d) What makes a modern computer image better than a standard TV image?

4. a) Many computer monitors are available today. Some have more pixels per centimeter than others. Why is the number of pixels per centimeter important?
   b) Would you prefer a monitor with more pixels per centimeter or with fewer? Explain why.

5. a) Suppose you observe a still black-and-white picture on a computer screen. The screen has about half a million pixels. Each of those pixels is stored inside the computer as a one or a zero. Now the picture suddenly bursts into color. Which image requires more memory? How much more? Explain your answer.
   b) Now the picture comes to life as full-motion color video. Which requires more memory, the still image or the video? Explain your answer.

6. a) A traveling spaceship can send back binary messages. Describe how these messages might be made into an image.
   b) If you could send one image to an extraterrestrial, which image would you choose?
   c) How would you transmit it?
   d) What would the extraterrestrial have to know to turn your digital message back into the picture?

7. a) How much time would it take to transmit a digital picture?
   b) Estimate the number of zeroes and ones that you would need.
   c) Select a total time for transmitting the picture.
   d) Estimate the rate of transmission (in zeroes and ones per second) that you would need to send the message in this time.

STRETCHING EXERCISES

Find some images from the Hubble Space Telescope. These images can be found at the NASA site on the world-wide web. The original image from the telescope was recorded digitally. It was transmitted to Earth digitally. Sometimes these images are processed by a computer to make them look smoother. Find a smoothed image that you can compare with the original image. Describe the differences.

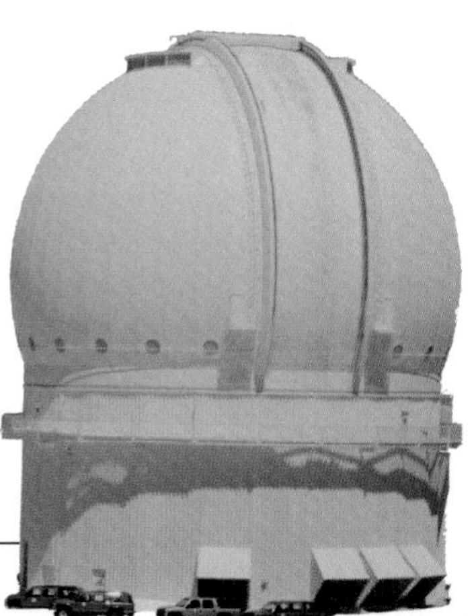

Activity Four

The Electromagnetic Spectrum

WHAT DO YOU THINK?

News reports are often sent from reporters at a distant location to network headquarters by satellite. The report goes from Earth to a satellite and then back to Earth. When you watch the news, you can observe a delay between the end of a question from the anchor and the beginning of the reporter's answer.

- **What causes this delay?**

Record your ideas about this question in your *Active Physics log*. Be prepared to discuss your responses with your small group and with your class.

FOR YOU TO DO

1. The table lists three different kinds of electromagnetic radiation. Next to each is the antenna, detector, or enclosure for that kind of radiation. Estimate the size of each of the three devices mentioned.

   a) Record your estimate in the appropriate column in a table in your log.

Kind of electromagnetic wave	Antenna/ enclosure	Size of antenna/ enclosure	Estimated wavelength	Estimated frequency
Radar	Radar gun			
Microwave	Microwave oven			
Radio	Telescoping antenna			

2. Assume that the wavelength of the electromagnetic radiation is about the same size as the antenna or enclosure given in the table. Make an estimate of each wavelength.

   a) Record your estimate in the table.

3. Wave speed, frequency, and wavelength are related by this equation.

$$\text{speed} = \text{frequency} \times \text{wavelength}$$

In mathematical language:

$$v = f\lambda$$

where v = speed

f = frequency

λ = wavelength

   a) Solve this equation for the frequency (f). Record this equation in your log.

   b) Find the frequency (f) for each of the three kinds of radiation. You will need the speed of light, which is $c = 3.0 \times 10^8$ m/s. Record your result in the table. See the sample calculation for FM radio on the next page.

Example:

An FM radio antenna on a car is approximately 1 m long. Therefore, assume that FM radio waves have a wavelength of 1 m.

$$f = \frac{v}{\lambda}$$

$$f = \frac{3 \times 10^8 \text{ m/s}}{1 \text{ m}}$$

$$f = 3 \times 10^8 \text{ Hz}$$

4. Listen to a recording of communication between the Apollo astronauts on the moon and Mission Control on Earth. Listen closely when someone asks a question and then receives an answer. This communication took place with radio waves. The question traveled by radio from Earth to the moon. After it reached the moon, the astronauts gave the answer. The answer traveled by radio to Earth. On Earth, there was a delay observed between the end of the question and the beginning of the answer. Estimate this time delay.

   a) Make several estimates, record each, and take the average.

   b) From the time delay you found in part (a), calculate the distance the radio waves traveled. The speed of light is 3×10^8 m/s. You can find the distance using this equation:

   Distance = speed × time

   $$d = vt$$

   In this case:

   d = the distance the radio waves travel

   v = the speed of the radio waves

   t = the time of the delay

c) The distance you calculated is the round-trip distance of the radio waves. Calculate the one-way distance (the distance between the Earth and the moon).

d) When the Voyager spacecraft was on its journey to Jupiter, there was a ninety-minute delay between sending a signal from Earth and receiving a response. How far away was the spacecraft?

FOR YOU TO READ

Calculating the Speed of Light

About 400 years ago, Galileo tried to measure the speed of light. He had no instruments, not even a clock. Galileo stood on a hilltop. He uncovered a lantern and began counting. When his assistant on a distant hilltop saw the light from Galileo's lantern, the assistant uncovered his lantern. When Galileo saw the assistant's lantern, he stopped counting. Galileo realized immediately that the speed of light was too large to measure in this way.

Although Galileo did not succeed in measuring the speed of light, he did recognize that light takes time to move from one place to another. That meant light has a speed. Galileo inspired others to try this measurement. Roemer succeeded about seventy years later. He viewed Jupiter's moons. By making observations at two different positions of the Earth's orbit, he was able to increase the total time the light traveled. He measured this larger time accurately. An American, Albert Michelson, made an accurate measurement with rotating mirrors. For his work he won the Nobel prize, the first ever awarded to an American scientist.

PHYSICS TALK

Electromagnetic Waves

Electromagnetic waves include radio, television, microwaves, infrared, visible, ultraviolet, X-rays, gamma rays and radar. They share many properties. All can travel through a vacuum. All travel at the same incredible speed, 3×10^8 m/s (186,000 mi. per sec.). This is so fast that if you could set up mirrors in New York and Los Angeles, and bounce a light beam back and forth, it would make 30 round trips in just one second!

REFLECTING ON THE ACTIVITY AND THE CHALLENGE

In this activity you have learned about the electromagnetic spectrum. Scientists have learned about the universe through observations of electromagnetic waves. You have been told that all the different kinds of electromagnetic waves have the same speed. You have also learned about the speed of light. The most likely way to communicate with extraterrestrial life is through sending and receiving electromagnetic radiation. You can use what you have learned in this activity when you design a plan to look and listen for life in space.

PHYSICS TO GO

1. Explain why Galileo was unable to make a measurement of the speed of light.

2. a) In step 2 of the activity, you assumed that the detector of electromagnetic radiation is about the same size as the wavelength of the radiation. The light-sensitive cells in the eye have a diameter of about 1.0×10^{-6} m. From this diameter, estimate the wavelength of visible light.

   b) From your answer to part (a), estimate the frequency of visible light.

3. a) Look at the list of electromagnetic waves.

Type of Wave	Typical Frequency
AM radio	1 MHz (10^6 Hz)
FM radio/commercial TV	100 MHz
radar	1 GHz (10^9 Hz)
microwaves	10 GHz
infrared radiation	10^{12} Hz
light	6 x 10^{14} Hz
ultraviolet radiation	10^{16} Hz
X-rays	10^{18} Hz
gamma rays	10^{21} Hz

   b) Calculate the wavelength of each type of wave.

4. a) The table shows some astronomical distances in meters. For each distance, calculate how long it takes light to go that distance.

From—To	Distance (meters)
Earth to moon	3.8×10^{8}
Earth to sun	1.5×10^{11}
sun to Pluto	5.9×10^{12}
sun to nearest star	4.1×10^{16}

   b) You can use the travel time of light as a unit of distance. For instance, the distance from the Earth to the moon is 1.3 light-seconds. Convert the distance from the Earth to the sun to light-minutes. To do this, find the number of minutes it takes light to reach the Earth from the sun.
   c) Convert the distance from the sun to Pluto to light-hours. You need to divide the time in your table by the number of seconds in an hour.
   d) Large astronomical distances are measured in light-years. This is the distance light travels in one year. Convert the distance from the sun to the next-nearest star to light-years.
   e) If a spacecraft could go almost as fast as the speed of light, how much time would it take to travel to the next nearest star?

5. a) Think back to how Galileo attempted to measure the speed of light. How much time did it take the light to travel from one hilltop to the other? Assume that the hill was 5 km away.
   b) Could Galileo have measured the speed of light with this method? Explain your answer.

6. Do you think that an extraterrestrial would be able to "see" with the same light that you do? If you learned that extraterrestrials could see microwaves, what might that tell you about their "eyes?" Draw an extraterrestrial who can see microwaves. Also draw one that can see radio waves.

7. How could you choose a frequency that beings on a planet in a distant galaxy might be listening to? How would you know?

STRETCHING EXERCISES

1. You can measure the speed of sound in the same way that Galileo tried to measure the speed of light. Remember, though, that sound is not part of the electromagnetic spectrum. You and your partner will need a pair of cymbals and a stopwatch. Stand as far apart as possible. Time how long it takes for the sound of the crash of the cymbals to travel the distance between you and your partner. Remember that you can see the crash.

2. Ultraviolet radiation from the sun can be dangerous to your skin and eyes. Research this problem and make a report to the class.

Activity Five

Interference and Spectra

WHAT DO YOU THINK?

All of the nuclei in your body were created in stars.

- **How can astronomers figure out what kind of atoms are in stars?**

Record your ideas about this question in your *Active Physics log*. Be prepared to discuss your responses with your small group and with your class.

FOR YOU TO DO

1. View a white light through a diffraction grating. Repeat the experiment for a different grating.The grating contains very fine parallel lines. Try to view these lines under a microscope.

   a) Draw a sketch in your log of the patterns produced by your grating.

2. Mount the grating in the laser beam. Mount the screen several meters away from the grating, as shown. Observe the pattern of spots on the screen.

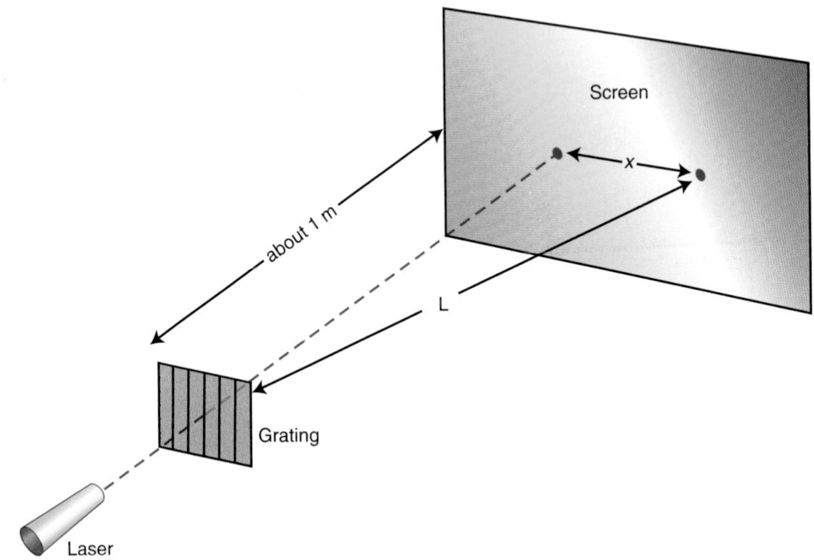

Never look directly at a laser beam or shine a laser beam into someone's eyes. Always work above the plane of the beam and beware of reflections from shiny surfaces.

a) Measure and record the separation between one spot and the next, x.

b) Measure and record the distance from the grating to the screen, L.

c) Measure and record the spacing between the lines of the grating, d. Alternately, you can use the spacing given by the manufacturer.

3. From your measurements, find the wavelength of the light. You will use the following equation

$$\lambda = \frac{d\,x}{L}$$

where λ is the wavelength of laser light

L is the distance from the grating to the spot on the screen
x is the separation between the spots
d is the spacing between lines in the grating

a) Show your calculations in your log.

4. Set aside the laser. Fasten the grating to the end of a cardboard tube or film can. Place a slit at the other end, as shown. Be sure the slit lines up with the grating. You have made a spectroscope.

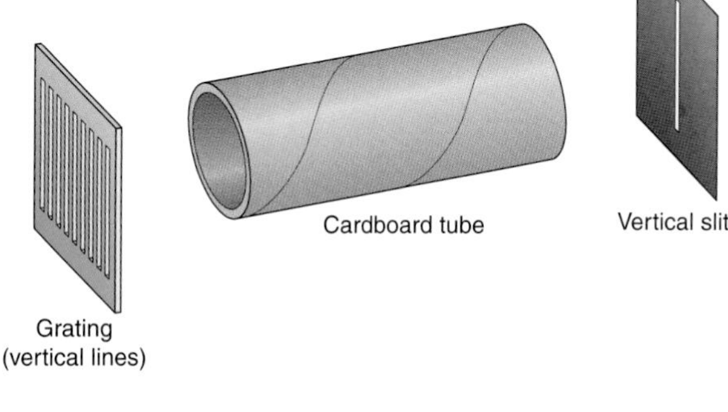

5. Aim your spectroscope at a white light source with the grating toward your eye. What you see is called a *spectrum*.

   a) Sketch the spectrum you see.

   b) White light makes a continuous spectrum. "Continuous" means going on smoothly without a break. How well does "continuous" describe what you see? Explain your answer.

6. With your spectroscope, view the light of several spectrum tubes (hydrogen, mercury, neon, and helium).

   a) Sketch what you see for each element.

   b) What do all these spectra have in common? How is each spectrum different?

7. Measure the wavelength of two of the lines you see in your spectroscope. You will view the spectrum by looking through the grating. Stand about one meter from the tube. Have your partner stand beside the spectrum tube and face you. Be sure you can see the spectrum tube. Your partner will move a finger of one hand outward until it lines up with one of the spectral lines.

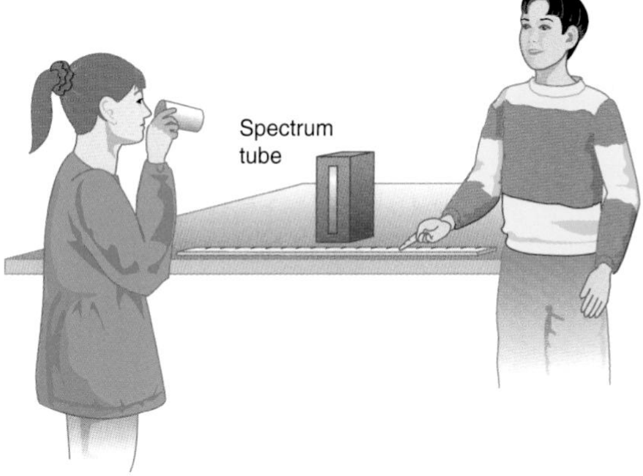

   a) Measure and record the distance between your partner's finger and the spectrum tube. This will be the value of x you will use in the equation:

$$\lambda = \frac{d\,x}{L}$$

b) Measure and record the distance between the grating and the spectral line. This will be the value of L you will use in the equation.

c) Calculate the value of the wavelength of this spectral line.

d) Repeat the above calculation for another spectral line.

8. Bite into a wintergreen mint, cracking it into pieces, while your lab partners watch for flashes of light. These mints have the interesting property of giving off flashes of light when they are crushed. The molecules themselves break up, and as they do, they give off light. The light is characteristic of the molecule.

FOR YOU TO READ

Spectra: The Fingerprints of Elements

You have observed the bright spectral lines of hydrogen. Hydrogen can give off light of these colors. Hydrogen can also absorb light of these colors. In that case, you would observe the entire spectrum with thin black lines missing. Either way, these specific colors are evidence of hydrogen.

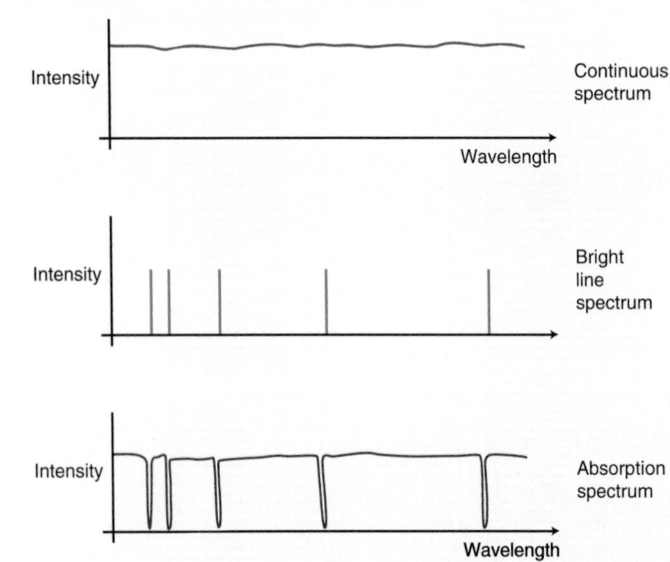

Each different gas gives off a particular kind of light. The spectroscope creates a line spectrum, which shows groups of lines of different wavelengths. The pattern of the lines is a fingerprint for the kind of atom that produced the light. No two people have the same fingerprints, and no two unlike atoms have the same set of spectral lines.

Astronomers use this spectrum to identify those chemical elements present in the outer part of the star. The elements astronomers have identified in stars are the same elements known on Earth. When astronomers analyzed the spectrum of the Sun, they found a set of lines from hydrogen. But there was another set of lines that was a puzzler, because these lines had never been observed on Earth. These lines came from the element helium, and at that time helium had not yet been discovered on Earth. The new element was named after Helios, the Greek sun god. Of course, scientists soon discovered that helium was indeed present on the Earth as well.

REFLECTING ON THE ACTIVITY AND THE CHALLENGE

In this activity, you have learned how a diffraction grating separates white light into light of all the colors of the rainbow. You have learned that scientists use gratings to reveal the characteristic spectral lines of gases. These lines enable astronomers to identify the gases that are present on stars. You have also learned that there are two different types of spectra—emission spectra and absorption spectra. Emission spectra consist of bright lines, the kind you saw through the spectroscope. Absorption spectra consist of dark lines, the kind in the spectrum of a star. The spectral lines would be known by any advanced civilization and could be the basis of a common language. You can use what you have learned to plan communication with extraterrestrial life

PHYSICS TO GO

1. a) Take your spectroscope home and use it to view the spectra of any and all lights or colors you might see. Street lights and lighted signs in store windows are highly recommended.
   b) Some colors are rather "washed out," while others are very "pure" (saturated). Can you explain the difference with the data you obtain from your spectrometer?
2. How might spectra be used to communicate with an extraterrestrial?
3. a) How might spectra be used for receiving communication from an extraterrestrial?
   b) Would spectra information be a common "language" for two civilizations?
4. a) Many spectral lines are not in the visible light range. How are such lines detected and measured?
   b) In communicating with an extraterrestrial, which spectral lines would you send?
   c) If the spectral lines you received from an extraterrestrial were in the infrared, what might this tell you about the intelligent life form?

5. All elements and compounds have their own characteristic spectra. Spectra can identify which element or compound is present, even when very little is present. For instance, tiny amounts of substances that are dissolved in water cannot be detected by chemical tests. But scientists can analyze the spectra of the solution to find out what is in the solution. For example, spectra can be used to investigate:
   - toxins in food
   - chemical spills in a river
   - a drug overdose in an unconscious victim

   How could the information from the spectra be used in each case?

6. a) The Delaney clause in the Pure Food and Water Act states that no food can be sold that contains any carcinogen (cancer-causing chemical). It doesn't matter how small the amount of the chemical is, even if it is only a trace. In fact, trace amounts (tiny concentrations) of carcinogens are believed to be harmless. At the time this act was passed, there was no way to test for trace substances, since the spectral analysis had not yet been developed. But now, with spectra, these tiny concentrations can be identified. So because of this law, food could be taken off the market, even though scientists believe it is perfectly safe. Discuss how the government should deal with this conflict.

   b) The Delaney clause was changed in 1996! Research this change and describe some of the foods affected by the change. Do you think they are safe to eat?

STRETCHING EXERCISES

1. Set up two identical loudspeakers about 1 m apart. Send the same 1000 Hz sine wave from an oscillator to each speaker. Walk around and investigate the changes in loudness. The places where the sound is loud corresponds to the bright spots when using light. This experiment is the audio version of the interference experiment you performed in this activity.

2. Research the field of electronic noise cancellation. Make a report to the class on how it works.

Activity Six

Send Them a Recording

WHAT DO YOU THINK?

Today you can buy an entire encyclopedia on a compact disc.

- **Is there any limit to how much can be stored on a single disc?**

Record your ideas about this question in your *Active Physics log*. Be prepared to discuss your responses with your small group and with your class.

FOR YOU TO DO

1. Carefully place a pin through the bottom of a Styrofoam® cup. Gently let the pin ride in the groove of a long-playing record, as shown in the drawing.

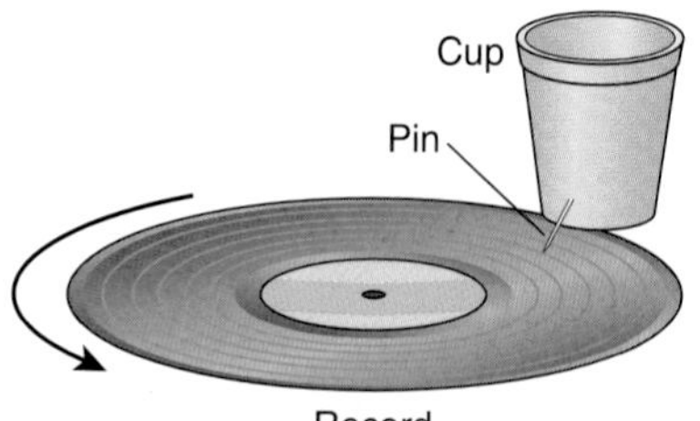

a) What do you hear?

2. Examine the grooves of the record with a magnifier.
   a) In your log, make a sketch of what you see.
   b) How do you think the grooves represent the sound?

3. Place a centimeter ruler on the record, so the ruler extends out from the center. Estimate the grooves in one centimeter of the record.
   a) Record your estimate in your log.

4. Another way to estimate the number of grooves in a centimeter of record is by timing how long it takes to play a one-centimeter band of the record. Read the example below.
   a) Use this method to make an estimate for your record.

Example:

The number of revolutions per minute is $33\frac{1}{3}$. (This was determined by the manufacturer of the record.)

$$\text{Number of revolutions/second} = \left(\frac{\text{number of revolutions}}{\text{min}}\right)\left(\frac{1\text{ min}}{60\text{ s}}\right)$$

$$= \left(\frac{33\frac{1}{3}\text{ rev}}{\text{min}}\right)\left(\frac{1\text{ min}}{60\text{ s}}\right)$$

$$= 0.56\ \frac{\text{rev}}{\text{s}}$$

Suppose the time to play 1 cm is 150 s.

$$\text{Number of revolutions in 1 cm} = 0.56\text{ rev/s} \times 150\text{ s}$$

$$= 84\text{ rev}$$

The number of grooves per centimeter is about 84.

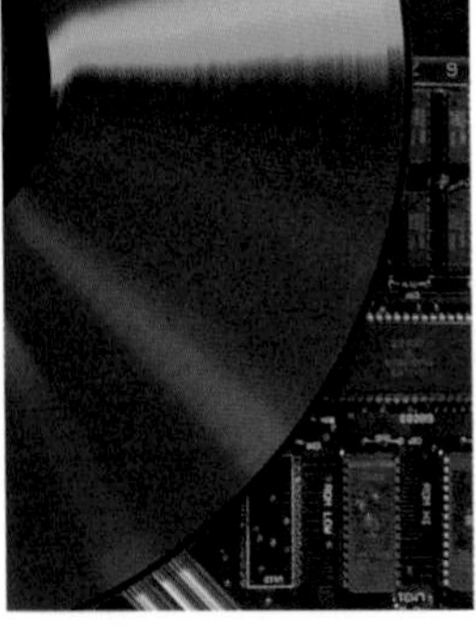

5. There is a third way to find the number of grooves per centimeter. This way uses interference of light, which you investigated in Activity Five. You will need a laser pointer. Tape a white piece of paper to a wall to be the screen. Mount a $33\frac{1}{3}$ rpm record 100 cm from the screen as shown in the diagram. You can lean the record against a stack of books.

6. Mount the laser pointer on books so the beam hits the record and is reflected to the screen.
   a) What do you see on the screen?
   b) Measure and record the distance between two of the central dots.

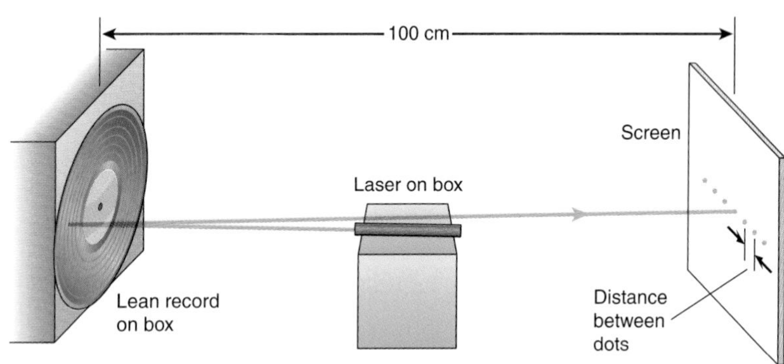

7. Use the example below.

Example:

The distance d between the grooves can be found by using the equation:

$$\lambda = \frac{d\,x}{L} \quad \text{or} \quad d = \frac{\lambda L}{x}$$

where $\lambda = 6.7 \times 10^{-5}$ cm

$L = 100$ cm

x = distance between the dots

Assume that $x = 0.5$ cm

$$\text{Then } d = \frac{6.7 \times 10^{-5}\text{ cm} \times 100\text{ cm}}{0.5\text{ cm}}$$

$$= 0.0134\text{ cm}$$

$$\text{Number of grooves/cm} = \frac{1}{d} = \frac{1}{0.0134} = 75$$

   a) Calculate the number of grooves per centimeter using this method.
   b) How does this calculated value compare with what you found using the first two methods?

Never look directly at a laser beam or shine a laser beam into someone's eyes. Always work above the plane of the beam and beware of reflections from shiny surfaces.

8. Suppose you unwound all the grooves in the 1-cm band you have been investigating so you had a groove that made a straight line, as shown.
   a) Estimate how long this groove would be.
   b) You have already found the number of grooves in the band. If you can find the distance around a typical groove (its circumference), then you can find the total length of the groove. Use the equation for circumference: $C = \pi d$

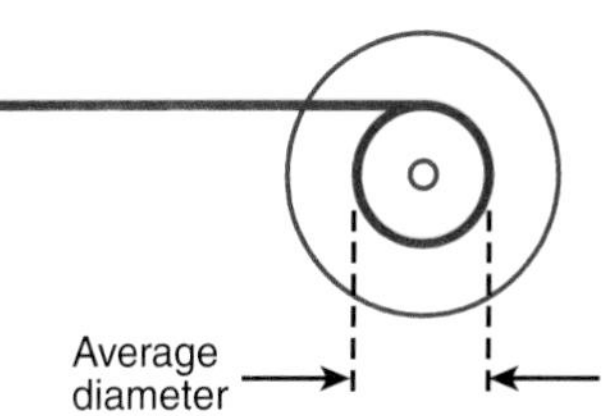

Average circumference = $\pi \times$ average diameter

9. Examine a CD. Observe the surface with a magnifier.
   a) What do you see? Do you see grooves?

10. Set up the laser pointer, screen, and CD as you did with the record. You will need a much wider screen this time. Be sure that the CD is 100 cm from the screen.
    a) Measure and record the distance between the dots.
    b) Calculate the number of grooves per centimeter.
    c) How does your number of grooves per centimeter for the CD compare with what you found for the long-playing record? How many times larger is it?

11. Edison made the first grooved recording in 1877. It had about 25 grooves/cm and was a cylinder. In 1887 the record was a disk, played at 78 rpm, and had about 60 grooves/cm. Around 1950 the 33 $\frac{1}{3}$ rpm and 45 rpm records had about 80 grooves/cm. In 1958, stereo records appeared with about 110 grooves/cm. In 1982 came the first CD, with over 5,000 grooves/cm.
    a) Graph this data, with time on the horizontal axis.
    b) Look at the graph and think about how compressed recordings will become in the future. What do you think will happen?

FOR YOU TO READ

Analog and Digital Representation of Sound

The CD uses a completely different technology to store information than does the long-playing record. The long-playing record contained waves in its grooves. These grooves vibrate a needle and produce sound. When the music is loud, the wave amplitude is large. This is an *analog* representation of sound. The result is a smooth, continuous signal, like the one shown.

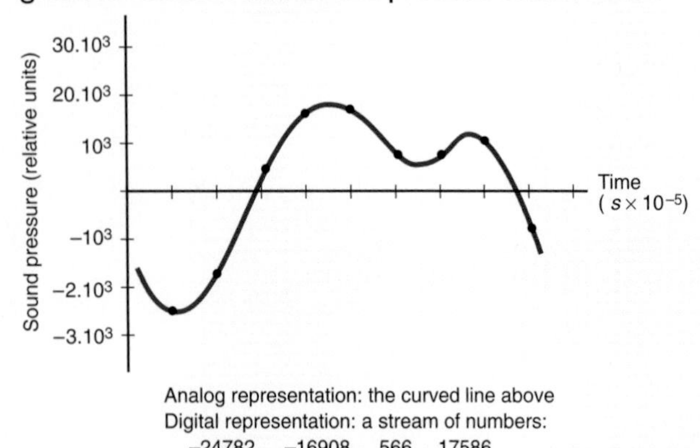

Analog representation: the curved line above
Digital representation: a stream of numbers:
–24782 –16908 566 17586
18694 860 832 11425

The CD provides a *digital* representation. The sound is represented by tiny black pits. A laser beam is aimed at the surface of the CD. If the pit is present, there is no reflection. If there is no pit, the beam is reflected. In the binary system, reflection produces a one. No reflection produces a zero. When the CD is originally recorded, an electronic device samples the sound about 40,000 times each second. These values are converted to binary numbers. They are then recorded on the CD as a stream of pits. The resulting signal looks like the one shown under the diagram.

When the CD plays, the player creates a long string of ones and zeroes. Computer technology in the CD player turns this stream of data into very high-quality audio signals.

REFLECTING ON THE ACTIVITY AND THE CHALLENGE

In this activity you have learned about the way information is stored on long-playing records and compact disks. You have explored three different methods to calculate the number of grooves per centimeter on the long-playing record. You have learned that the analog recording on a long-playing record uses a smooth, continuous groove to represent the vibrations of the sound. The CD, on the other hand, is a record of a sampling of the sound. The samples are stored as tiny pits, which provide a digital recording. You have discovered that there are far more grooves per centimeter in the CD than in the long-playing record. You can use what you have learned to plan a recording to send into space to communicate with extraterrestrials. You can decide if the recording should be analog or digital, and you can explain the physics behind your decision.

PHYSICS TO GO

1. a) Explain how sound is stored on a long-playing record.
   b) Explain how sound is stored on a CD.

2. a) What is analog recording?
   b) What is digital recording?
   c) Explain how a long-playing record is an analog recording.
   d) Explain how a CD is a digital recording.

3. a) Is a clock with hands analog or digital? Give a reason for your answer.
   b) Is a clock with only numbers analog or digital? Give a reason for your answer.

4. a) Estimate the length of a popular song in seconds.
   b) A CD samples the sound 40,000 times a second. How many samples are in a popular song?
   c) Each sample represents the loudness at that instant. Eight ones or zeroes are needed to represent the loudness. How many ones and zeroes are needed to represent the whole song?

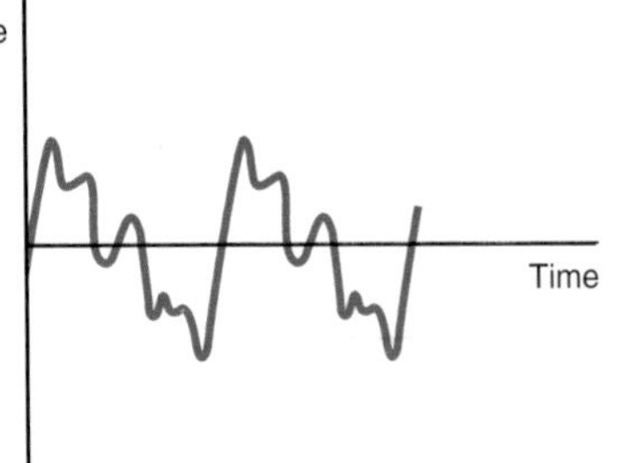

5. a) The drawing shows the waveform of a note on a guitar. Is this waveform an analog or a digital representation of the sound? Explain how you found your answer.
   b) How would you make a digital representation of this sound?

6. a) When a CD is made, the sound is sampled 40,000 times per second. How long is the time between samples?
   b) What is the frequency range of human hearing?
   c) What is the highest frequency that you think would be recorded on a CD?
   d) What is the period of this frequency? Hint: The period is the time for one cycle of the sound.
   e) If the sampling rate is 40,000 times per second, will that give an accurate representation of this high-frequency sound? Explain your reasoning.

7. When you play a CD, 40,000 sound samples per second come out of the speaker. Why doesn't the music sound choppy?

8. a) What advantages do CDs have over long-playing records?
   b) Do records have any advantages over CDs?

9. If a groove on a record is damaged, the needle skips and the sound is distorted. What can go wrong with a CD?

10. What advances in CD technology do you expect in the next ten years?

11. a) You are in charge of creating a recording about our civilization. The recording will be sent into space. How much information can you include on such a record?
    b) What information might you include?
    c) How would you provide instructions for using the record player or CD player?

STRETCHING EXERCISE

Go to the NASA web site and search for information about the Voyager program. Report to the class on the records that were placed aboard the Voyager spacecraft.

Activity Seven

The Size of Space

WHAT DO YOU THINK?

If you have normal eyesight, your eyes can read a book or see across a stadium.

- **How do your eyes and brain estimate distances in order to focus properly?**

Record your ideas about this question in your *Active Physics log*. Be prepared to discuss your responses with your small group and with your class.

FOR YOU TO DO

1. Hold your index finger out at arm's length. With one eye closed or covered, line up your index finger with a distant object. You are "sighting" the object. Without moving your index finger, close or cover the other eye instead. What happens to your view of the distant object?

   a) In your log explain what happened.

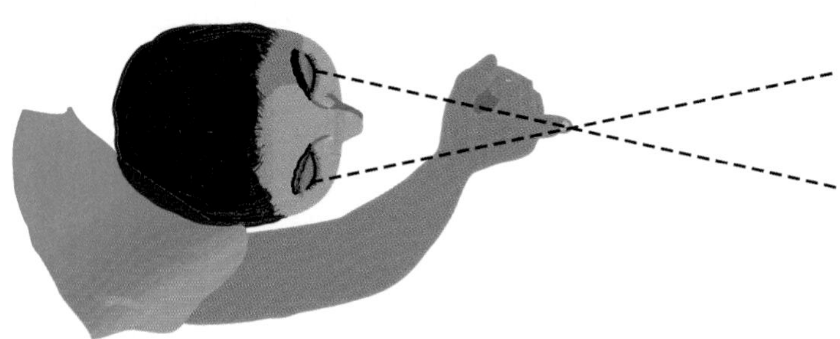

You sighted your finger first from one eye and then from the other. This shift in the position of your finger compared to the distant object is called *parallax*.

2. You can use parallax to find the distance to an object in your lab. You will sight an object from two different places, just as you did in step 1. Find an object on a wall, and stand as far back from it as possible. Mark the place where you are standing. As you sight this object, put a little tape on the floor to show the direction of the object.

3. Now move five meters sideways (that is, parallel to the wall). Again, mark the place where you are standing. Sight the object, and again put tape on the floor to show the direction you are sighting. The line between the two sighting places is called the baseline.

4. Measure the angles between the baseline and the two sight lines, which you marked with tape.

   a) Make a scale drawing on graph paper of the triangle made by the baseline and the two sight lines. Hint: First make a rough sketch of the triangle. This sketch will help you select a scale that will show the whole triangle on your graph paper.

5. Find the sides of the triangle from the scale drawing. Then measure the lengths of these sides directly.

   a) Record your measurements in your log. How accurate was your parallax measurement?

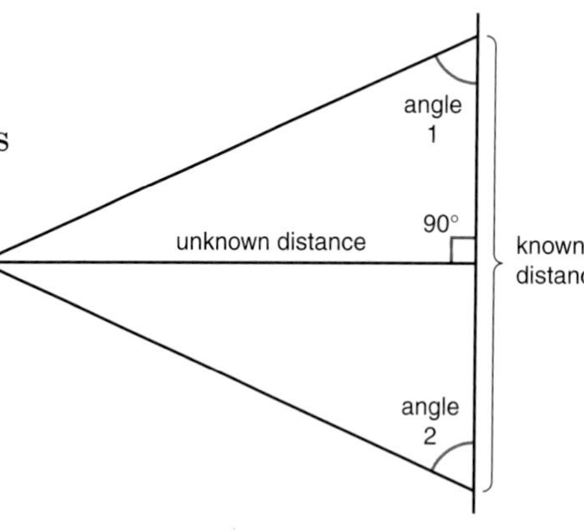

6. If possible, go outside to perform the same activity. This time, stand about 100 m from the object in an area free of traffic. Make the baseline at least 20 m. As before, measure the distance using parallax. Then measure the distance directly and compare your results.

   a) Record your measurements and results in your log.

PHYSICS TALK

Astronomers use parallax to measure the distances to nearby stars. The baseline is the diameter of the Earth's orbit, which is 3.0×10^{11} m. As the drawing shows, a telescope makes two sightings of the star. The sightings are six months apart, so the Earth will have moved halfway around the sun between the sightings.

The star is observed against the background of much more distant stars. From one sighting to the next, the star shifts slightly. This shift is very tiny, even though the baseline is so large.

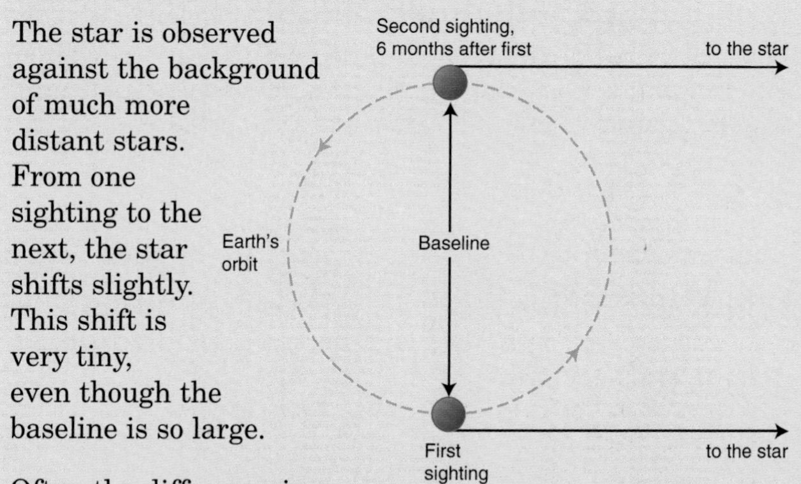

Often the difference in the two angles is only a few thousandths of a degree. With these angles, astronomers in essence construct a triangle by using trigonometry to find the distance with parallax, just as you did in this activity. The star with the greatest parallax shift is the nearest star, Proxima Centauri, which is 4.3 light-years away (or 4.1×10^{16} m) away.

REFLECTING ON THE ACTIVITY AND THE CHALLENGE

You have learned how astronomers measure the distances to nearby stars. These distances are important because you would have to travel at least that far to find extraterrestrial life. You can also use these distances in describing how you could communicate with light or radio, which travel at the speed of light. To reach the nearest star, a light beam or radio wave would require 4.3 years.

PHYSICS TO GO

1. a) Explain the concept of parallax.
   b) If you shift the position of your view, why does the position of a nearby object seem to shift?
   c) If you shift the position of your view, why does the position of a very distant object not seem to shift?
   d) Explain why astronomers cannot use parallax to calculate the distance to stars that are very far away.
   e) When you observed parallax in your lab, you observed how something nearby seemed to shift its position compared to an object on a distant wall. When an astronomer observes the shift in the position of a star, how can the astronomer tell that the star shifted? You used an object on a distant wall to observe a shift. What does the astronomer use?

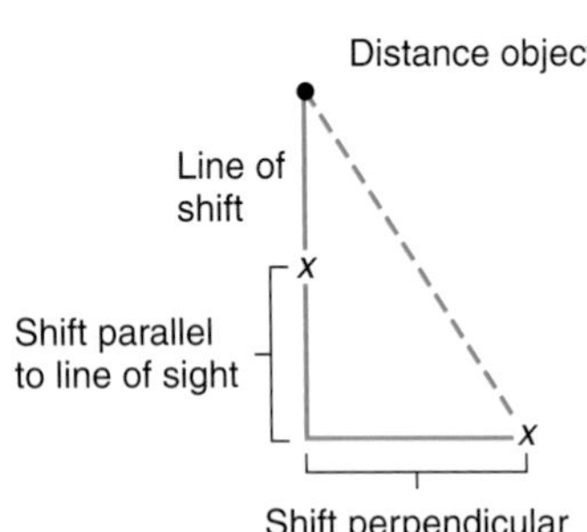

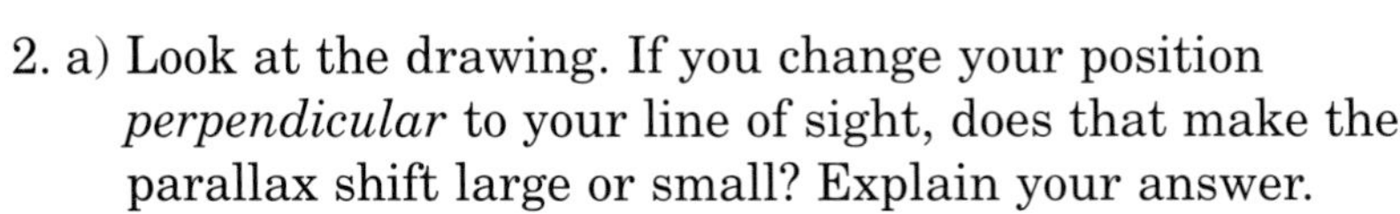

2. a) Look at the drawing. If you change your position *perpendicular* to your line of sight, does that make the parallax shift large or small? Explain your answer.
   b) Look at the drawing. If you change your position *parallel* to your line of sight, does that make the parallax shift large or small? Explain your answer.

3. a) Hold a pencil about 20 cm away. Look at the pencil through first one eye and then the other.
   b) What happens to the position of the pencil when you change from one eye to the other?
   c) Make a drawing to explain what happens.
   d) What happens if you look at the pencil through both eyes? What can you see with both eyes that you cannot see with just one?
   e) If you held the pencil twice as far away, what would change? Try it and see.

4. a) In Question 3, your baseline was the distance between your eyes. Approximately what is this distance?
   b) Make a top-view drawing like the one shown. The drawing shows the pencil and your baseline. Also show the object you are sighting.
   c) Now double the pencil distance. Make a drawing for this larger distance. On your drawing, show the angle between the line-of-sight from your left eye and the line-of-sight from your right eye.
   d) Double the distance again, and again make a drawing. Show the angle between the two lines-of-sight.
   e) Make a general statement about how the distance of the object affects the angle between the two lines-of-sight.

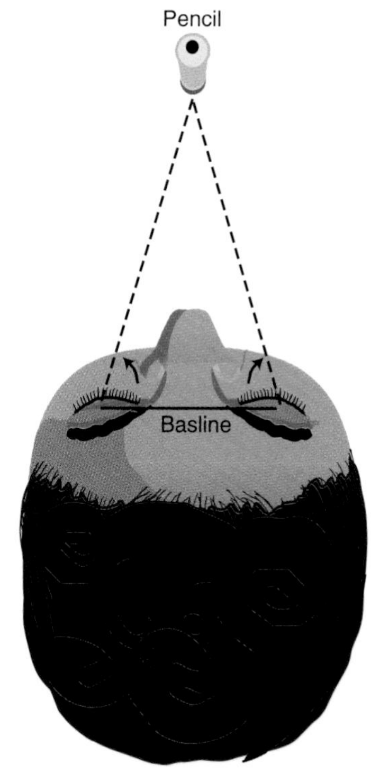

5. a) Depth perception is the ability to see how far away something is. Do you need both eyes for depth perception?
   b) Have someone hold a pencil about 30 cm in front of you. Cover or close one eye. Reach out and touch the pencil.
   c) Now look with both eyes. Reach out and touch the pencil.
   d) Was it easier to touch the pencil when you looked with both eyes or only with one? Tell why.

6. a) The speed of light is about 186,000 miles per second. About how many miles are in a light-year (i.e., the distance light travels in one year)? Hint: You will need to find the number of seconds in a year.
   b) If you could run five miles per hour, about how long would it take you to run a light-year?
   c) The speed of light is about 3×10^8 m/s. About how many meters are in a light-year?

STRETCHING EXERCISE

Visit a camera store that sells used cameras. Ask the salesperson to show you how a rangefinder camera works. Research rangefinders in the library and report what you have learned to your class.

Activity Eight

The Doppler Effect

WHAT DO YOU THINK?

You have probably heard the sound of a fast-moving car passing by you.

- **Why is there a change in tone as the car moves by?**

Record your ideas about this question in your *Active Physics log*. Be prepared to discuss your responses with your small group and with your class.

FOR YOU TO DO

1. Listen to a small battery-powered oscillator. It makes a steady tone with just one frequency. The oscillator is fastened inside a Nerf™ ball for protection.

2. Stand about 3 m away from your partner. Toss the oscillator back and forth between you. Listen to the pitch as the oscillator moves. As you listen, observe how the pitch changes as the oscillator moves.

   a) How is the oscillator moving when the pitch is the highest?

   b) How is the oscillator moving when the pitch is the lowest?

3. Stop the oscillator so you can listen to its "at rest" pitch.

   a) With the oscillator moving, record how the pitch has changed compared to the "at rest" pitch. How has the pitch changed when the oscillator is moving towards you?

   b) How has the pitch changed when the oscillator is moving away from you?

4. Look at the graph axes shown. The axes show pitch vs. velocity. When the velocity is positive, the oscillator is moving away from you. When the velocity is negative, the oscillator is moving towards you.

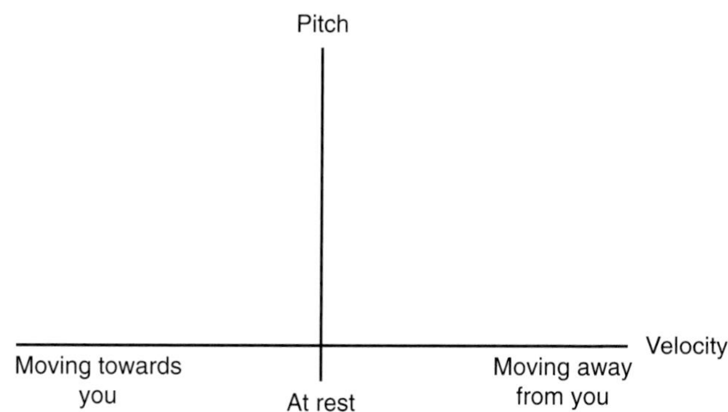

   a) On a similar set of axes in your log, sketch a graph of your pitch observations. Explain your graph to the other members of your group.

5. You can do an outdoor Doppler lab using the horn of a moving car as the wave source. Tape-record the horn when the car is at rest next to the tape recorder. Then, with the driver of the car maintaining an agreed-upon speed, tape the sound of the horn as the car passes. Have the driver blow the horn continuously, both as the car approaches and as it moves away. Be very careful to stay away from the path of the car.

6. You can determine the observed frequency by matching the recorded tone to the output of an oscillator and loudspeaker. Use this formula:

$$f = f_0\left(\frac{s}{(s-v)}\right)$$

f_0 = frequency when car is at rest

v = speed of the car

s = speed of sound = 340 m/s

a) When the car is moving toward you, v is positive. When the car is moving away from you, v is negative. Use the equation to calculate the speed of the car from the data you collected.

FOR YOU TO READ

Measuring Distances Using the Doppler Effect

Astronomers measure distances to stars in two different ways. One way is with parallax, but this method works only for the nearest stars. For all other stars astronomers use the Doppler shift of spectral lines. The next-nearest galaxy is Andromeda, more than a million light-years away. Astronomers have observed galaxies at far greater distances, up to about 12 billion light-years away. These incredible distances are measured by observation of the absorption lines, which you investigated in Activity Five. These lines are consistently Doppler-shifted towards the red end of the spectrum, and the result is called the "red shift."

All the lines are shifted toward longer wavelengths. Since this is a shift towards lower frequencies, the galaxies are moving away from us. By measuring the size of the shift, astronomers find the speed of distant galaxies. Different galaxies move away at different speeds, but with a clear pattern. The farther away the galaxy, the faster it is moving away, as shown in the graph.

Astronomers explain this result with the Big Bang theory, which says that the universe began in an explosion about 15 billion years ago. After the explosion, the matter in the galaxy continued to move apart, even after the galaxies formed.

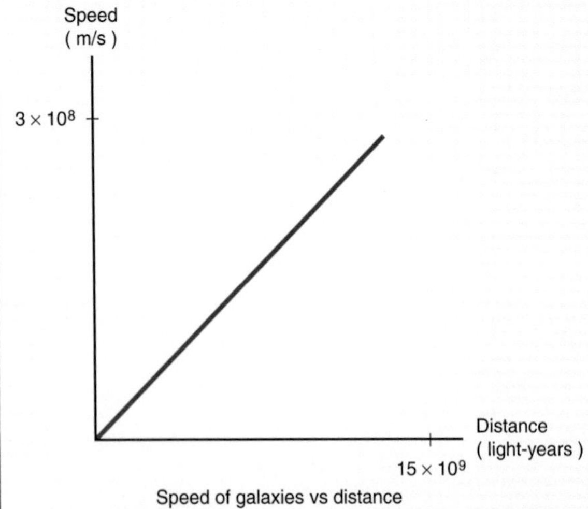

Speed of galaxies vs distance

REFLECTING ON THE ACTIVITY AND THE CHALLENGE

You now have learned how astronomers measure distances in the universe. They use parallax for nearby stars, and they use the Doppler effect for distant galaxies. Since there may be life in the distant galaxies, it is important to understand how far away they are. Since even the closest galaxy is more than a million light-years away, communicating with life from another galaxy will be a great challenge. You can use what you have learned to meet the chapter challenge, because you now can explain how the distances to galaxies are measured.

PHYSICS TO GO

1. a) If a sound source is moving towards an observer, what happens to the pitch the observer hears?
   b) If a sound source is moving towards an observer, what happens to the sound frequency the observer measures?

2. a) If a sound source is moving away from an observer, what happens to the pitch the observer hears?
   b) If a sound source is moving away from an observer, what happens to the sound frequency the observer measures?

3. a) If you watch an auto race on television, what do you hear as the cars go by the camera and microphone?
   b) Sketch a graph of the pitch you hear vs. time. Make the horizontal axis of your graph the time, and the vertical axis the pitch. Hint: Don't put any numbers on your axes. Label the time when the car is going right by you.
   c) Sketch a graph of the frequency you observe vs. time. As in part (b), label the time when the car is going right by you. Hint: Don't put any numbers on your axes.

4. a) In Question 3 above, what would happen to your graphs if the speed of the racing car doubled? Make a sketch to show the change.
   b) What would happen to your graphs if the speed of the racing car was cut in half? Make a sketch to show the change.

5. a) Red light has a longer wavelength than blue light. Which light has the lower frequency? You will need the equation:

   wave speed = wavelength × frequency

   Show how you found your answer.

   b) When the oscillator moved away from you, was the pitch you heard lower or higher?
   c) When the oscillator moved away from you, was the frequency you heard lower or higher?
   d) If light from a distant galaxy is shifted towards the red, is it shifted to a lower or a higher frequency?
   e) If the light is shifted towards the red, is the galaxy moving away from Earth or towards Earth?

STRETCHING EXERCISE

Watch a broadcast of an auto race. Listen closely to the cars as they zoom past the microphone. Use the Doppler effect to explain your observations.

Activity Nine

Communication Through Space

WHAT DO YOU THINK?

In 1865, Jules Verne wrote *From the Earth to the Moon*. In this book, a team of three astronauts were shot to the moon from a cannon in Florida. They returned by landing in the ocean. Verne correctly anticipated many of the details of the Apollo missions.

- **How well do you think Star Trek predicts the future?**

Record your ideas about this question in your *Active Physics log*. Be prepared to discuss your responses with your small group and with your class.

FOR YOU TO DO

1. Alexander Graham Bell's grandson suggested a simple way to talk to Europe long-distance. He recommended placing a long air tube across the bottom of the Atlantic Ocean. He believed that if someone spoke into one end of the tube, someone else at the other end would hear what was said.

   a) Do you think this is practical? Give reasons for your answer.

   b) If the sound could be heard in Europe, how long would it take to send a message? Hint: The distance to Europe is about 5000 km, and the speed of sound is about 340 m/s.

   c) Compare this time with the time to communicate with extraterrestrials in the next galaxy using light. The nearest galaxy is Andromeda, which is about two million light-years away (It takes light about two million years to get from Earth to Andromeda).

2. The highest speed ever observed is the speed of light, 3×10^8 m/s. In addition, a basic idea of Einstein's Theory of Relativity is that no material body can move faster than light. Radio waves also travel at the speed of light. If Einstein is correct, there are serious limitations on communication with extraterrestrials. Look at the table of distances below. These are distances from the Earth.

to the Sun:	1.5×10^{11} m
to Jupiter:	8×10^{11} m
to Pluto:	6×10^{12} m
to the nearest star:	4×10^{16} m
to the center of our galaxy:	2.2×10^{20} m
to the Andromeda galaxy:	2.1×10^{22} m
to the edge of the observable universe:	1.5×10^{26} m

   a) How long would it take to send a message using radio waves to each place?

   b) How long would it take to send this message and get an answer back?

3. A real-life problem occurred when the Voyager spacecraft was passing the outer planets. NASA sent instructions to the spacecraft but had to wait a long time to find out what happened. The ship had to receive the instructions, take data, and send the data back home.
   a) If the spacecraft was at Jupiter, how long would it take for the message to travel back-and-forth?
   b) If this spacecraft was at Pluto, how long would it take for the message to travel back-and-forth?

4. Make a time-line of Earth history. For the scale of your time-line, make six evenly spaced marks.
   a) Label the time-line like the one shown.

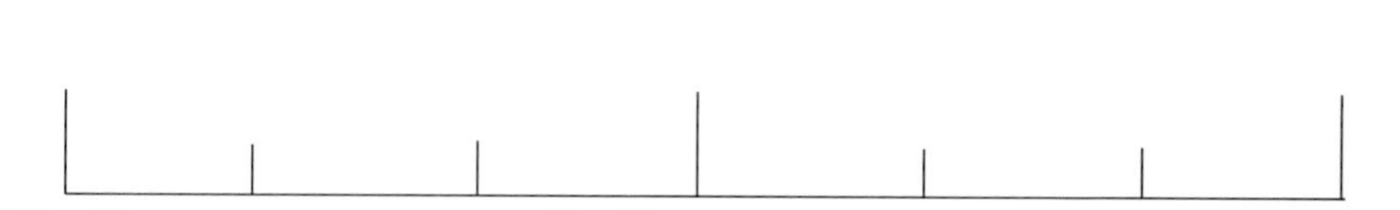

   b) On your time-line, label interesting events in Earth's history that occurred during these times. Possibilities include the end of the last Ice Age (10,000 years ago), the evolution of the modern horse (50 million years ago), the evolution of humans (3 million years ago), the Iron Age (1000 BC), the Stone Age (8000 BC), the Middle Ages in Europe (13th century), the beginning of civilization (3000 BC), and the spread of mammals over the Earth (50 million years ago).(Dates given are approximations.)

5. Many scientists believe that intelligent life would most likely be thousands or millions of light-years away.
   a) How would this affect two-way communication?
   b) If you asked a question, how long would it be before a response came back? Would you be able to receive the response?
   c) What questions would you ask? (Note: Think about the distances involved.)
   d) What kind of answers might you expect?
   e) What changes have occurred on Earth over this time period?
   f) What changes would you expect on Earth before the answer came?
   g) Is two-way communication possible over such distances? Is it practical? Is it likely?

REFLECTING ON THE ACTIVITY AND THE CHALLENGE

This activity has prepared you for at least two of the chapter challenges. You can now describe how the large distances in space would make communication difficult. You now know that you might not live long enough to receive any answer. What you have learned will be valuable for planning a way to communicate over a long period of time. Also, you have begun to think about what kind of message to send to another life form.

PHYSICS TO GO

1. a) The speed of sound is about 340 m/s in air. You and another student take gongs outside about 200 m apart. You hit the gong. After hearing the sound of your gong, the other student hits the other gong. How long is it before you hear the sound of the other gong?
   b) How is this experiment similar to the problem of communicating with extraterrestrial life?

2. a) If extraterrestrial life is probably 1,000 light-years away, would it be within this galaxy?
   b) If extraterrestrial life is likely probably several million light-years away, would that be within this galaxy? Could it be in the Andromeda galaxy? (Note: This galaxy has over 100 billion stars.)

3. a) The moon is 3.8×10^8 m from the Earth. How long does it take a radio wave to travel from the moon to the Earth?
   b) The sun is 1.5×10^{11} m from the Earth. How long does it take a light wave to travel from the sun to the Earth?
   c) Pluto is about 6×10^{12} m from the sun. How long does it take a light wave to travel from the sun to Pluto?
   d) The nearest star is 4.3 light-years away from Earth. How long does it take a radio wave to travel from Earth to the nearest star?
   e) This galaxy is about 100,000 light-years across. How long does it take light to go all the way across our galaxy?
   f) The nearest galaxy is more than a million light-years away. How long does it take light to reach us from this galaxy?
   g) The universe is about 15 billion light-years across. How long does it take light to cross the universe?

4. a) In Star Trek, the spaceship can move at "warp speed." This speed is faster than the speed of light. How is "warp speed" important for space travel?
   b) Do you think "warp drive" is likely to be developed? Is it possible? Explain your answers.
5. Suppose your job is to make a plan to send people in space ships to explore nearby galaxies. How would the distances in space affect your plan?
6. a) How would you choose a language for communication with extraterrestrials?
   b) Many scientists suggest that a good starting point is to describe the periodic table of the elements. Do you agree? Explain your answer.
   c) Is there any evidence that extraterrestrials would observe the same elements, with the same properties, that you observe? Tell what the evidence is.
   d) Do you think another advanced civilization would have already discovered the periodic table? Tell why or why not.
   e) How would you start to create a language?
   f) How would you begin communication?

7. a) Suppose that intelligent extraterrestrial beings exist. Suppose that you are able to communicate with them. Why would you want to?
   b) Should you be afraid of extraterrestrial beings?
   c) Is it more likely that they would help Earth or enslave Earth? (Note: Consider the distances involved.)
8. a) What is known of the Earth of 2,000 years ago?
   b) It takes 2,000 years for a spaceship to travel to a star. When the travelers arrive at the star, would their information about the Earth be up-to-date? Explain why or why not.
   c) If the trip to another star took 10,000 years, would such a trip be worthwhile? Explain why or why not.

9. A record was sent into space in an effort to communicate with extraterrestials.
   a) If you were on the team designing the record, what music would you include?
   b) What photographs would you include?
   c) What drawings would you include?
   d) Have you fairly represented the majority of the world with your choices?

10. a) Make a list of movies, books, and TV shows that involve trips to other parts of the galaxy or extraterrestrials visiting the Earth.
    b) Very briefly describe the plot of the story.
    c) How accurately is science represented?

STRETCHING EXERCISE

1. Read the Carl Sagan book, *Contact*, or watch the movie. What features of the book and movie have you considered in this chapter? What features have been ignored?

2. Look up the messages that were placed on the Pioneer and Voyager spacecraft. Make a report to the class on how this plaque communicated information about humans.

PHYSICS AT WORK

Dr. Neil Tyson

Is there another planet out there with beings looking for us?

"Nearly all scientists agree there is a strong likelihood that there is life on other planets," says Dr. Neil Tyson, the director of the Hayden Planetarium at the Museum of Natural History in New York City and an astrophysicist at Princeton University. "Although communication with extraterrestrial life is not the research focus of most astrophysicists, discovering a planet with any life—simple algae even—would be exciting."

His focus has been to determine the "structure of our galaxy," a task which he compares to "an unborn child trying to figure out what his mother looks like." Dr. Tyson and his colleagues must look past The Milky Way, at other galaxies hundreds of light-years away in an effort to understand by comparison.

The effort to understand other galaxies and other planets may one day allow us to affect what happens on earth. "We look at Venus, a planet similar in size to Earth" says Dr. Tyson. "Why is it so hot ? Well, there was a runaway greenhouse effect. Why is there no water on Mars? There is evidence that there was water there at one time. What happened?" These are questions that astrophysicists will continue to explore by "pushing the limits of technology."

"We now know of more planets outside of our solar system than inside and they have all been discovered in this decade," claims Dr. Tyson. "When searching for a planet we look for the Doppler effect in the host star," he continues. "A planet and a star orbit around a common center of gravity and we notice the presence of the planet by the jiggling of the host star. This concept, and others, has been predicted for some time but only substantiated in this decade with the development of both high-powered telescopes and sensitive detectors."

As for communication with extraterrestrial life, Dr. Tyson describes it as "an interesting challenge." One of the most interesting parts of the challenge is the language in which to communicate. "Certainly not English," he says. "Science is something that would appear the most universal. The periodic table of elements, for instance. The symbols may be different but the organization may be something we have in common. Nothing, of course, is certain. It is literally a shot in the dark."

Chapter 3 Assessment

All the activities you have done in this chapter were designed to give you the information, knowledge, and understanding to complete the chapter challenge. With what you have learned, you will be able to:

Outline a plan for how you would communicate with extraterrestrial life forms you might discover.

Decide what to say to extraterrestrial beings using science that they can understand and presenting them with important information about human life and Earth.

Write an essay describing what could be learned from contact with extraterrestrial beings.

Participate in a mock hearing of the Space Committee of the United States Senate regarding a request from scientists for $3 billion for a project to search for extraterrestrial life forms.

What do you think? Is there anyone out there listening to your communication?

Review the criteria for grading which you and your class developed at the beginning of this chapter. Do you wish to further modify the suggested grading scheme?

Part 1:

Choice of methods to communicate: 40 points

Explanation of the science:

- correct statement of science concepts: 25 points
- how Chapter 3 activities present these concepts: 35 points

Part 2:

Choice of language for communication; discussion of how extraterrestrials will be able to understand the science:

- correct statement of science used in communication: 25 points
- how extraterrestrials might use the science in a message: 25 points
- Choice of message content: 25 points

Description of how the content is important: 25 points

Physics You Learned

Distances in the universe

Communication with extraterrestrial life

Light-years

Electromagnetic radiation

Interference of light

Spectra

Doppler shift

Red-shift

Concave and convex lenses

Real and virtual images

Focal length

Telescopes

Analog and digital

Digital images

Information storage

Communication

Index

Charts/Graphs/Tables